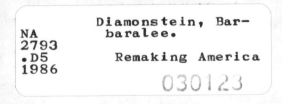

REMAKING AMERICA

ALSO BY BARBARALEE DIAMONSTEIN

Open Secrets: 94 Women in Touch with Our Time

Our 200 Years: Tradition and Renewal

The Art World: A Seventy-Five-Year Treasury of ARTnews

Inside New York's Art World

Buildings Reborn: New Uses, Old Places

American Architecture Now

Collaboration: Artists and Architects

Interior Design: The New Freedom

Vision and Images: American Photographers
on Photography

Handmade in America: Conversations with
Fourteen Craftmasters

American Architecture Now: Part II

Fashion: The Inside Story

NEW USES, OLD PLACES
REMAKING AMERICA

BARBARALEE DIAMONSTEIN

CROWN PUBLISHERS, INC. NEW YORK

Published by Crown Publishers, Inc.,
225 Park Avenue South, New York, New York, 10003
and represented in Canada by the Canadian MANDA Group
CROWN is a trademark of Crown Publishers, Inc.
Manufactured in Japan

Library of Congress Cataloging-in-Publication Data

Diamonstein, Barbaralee.
Remaking America.

Includes index.
1. Buildings—United States—Remodeling for other use.
I. Title.
NA2793.D5   1986   720'.28'60973   86-2650
ISBN 0-517-56287-1
10 9 8 7 6 5 4 3 2 1
First Edition

for Carl Spielvogel, a true original

CONTENTS

SOUTH

WEST

FOREWORD
BY PAUL GOLDBERGER

When Barbaralee Diamonstein's first book on adaptive reuse projects, *Buildings Reborn*, was published eight years ago, it had a mission very different from that of the present volume. That first book, and the traveling exhibition it was created to accompany, preached a relatively new gospel: the idea that our older buildings have lasting value, not only aesthetic but also economic and social, and that we are often much wiser to rehabilitate them than to tear them down.

It is at least in part a tribute to the success of that effort that that notion, once considered eccentric if not downright crazy, has by now become the common wisdom. It is no longer a radical idea to talk of saving older buildings, no longer an odd viewpoint to suggest that in many old buildings there may be whole new lives waiting to begin, and that these lives may even turn out to be more profitable economically than the buildings' previous ones. In the last decade the preservation and rehabilitation of older structures have become part of our culture. We have discovered—miracle of miracles—that we like older things, that they bring not only a degree of immediate visual pleasure that much modern architecture cannot offer, but also the deeper and more subtle gratifications of a sense of connection with the movements of time.

"In a city, time becomes visible," Lewis Mumford wrote many years ago, and he touched upon a critical need in any truly meaningful city, town, or village, the need to feel that the place was not created yesterday and will not be gone tomorrow. It is one thing to escape briefly into the time capsule of a futuristic Disneyland or a his-toric Williamsburg; it is quite another to attempt to live a real life, day in and day out, in a place so cut off from the continuum of time. Real places are enriched by their connections with the past; somehow this seems to prepare us better for the future, for it gives us the sense that the present is not some kind of bubble, floating free, but a real point in history.

Our culture's growing recognition of the values of preservation was helped along magnificently a few years back by enlightened tax laws which for the first time made it more beneficial to restore distinguished older buildings than to demolish them. These laws, which at this writing seem to have survived a threat to eliminate them in pending tax-reform legislation, have encouraged the very best kinds of historic preservation—not saving houses as quaint museums, but rehabilitating buildings for uses appropriate to the present time. The preservation-related tax credits now on the books have led to the conversion of so many fine commercial buildings into housing that they are now among the major sources of government housing finance—a triumphant vindication of the practical value of historic preservation.

The present tax laws have worked hand in hand with the growing social awareness that Barbaralee Diamonstein's earlier efforts have helped spark to make preservation and rehabilitation a truly national movement. And here is the special value of this new book on adaptive reuse, *Remaking America*. Here we see old buildings from all over the country, in large cities and small, from structures as widely known as the Old Post Office in Washington, D.C., to ones as obscure as the former railroad station and present library in White House Station, New Jersey. Some conversions are by celebrated architects, such as the Palladium nightclub in New York by Arata Isozaki and the Temporary Contemporary museum in Los Angeles by Frank Gehry. But others include an office in a former cemetery building in Indianapolis, a bookshop in a movie house in Houston, a hotel and retail complex in St. Louis's glorious Union Station, and many more. The movement spans the country, and almost every kind of building type.

For all the remarkable success of preservation efforts in recent years, however, the movement is far from invulnerable. Preservation has been put under particular pressure by the great real estate boom of the last couple of years; even though few critics would dare to suggest, as they did a generation ago, that preservation per se is point-less, there seems to be more and more eagerness to draw the line and to limit the reach of preservation efforts where they threaten the vast, overscaled developments that have become so commonplace.

This new pressure makes *Remaking America* all the more valuable right now. For taken as a group, the buildings described in these pages are the ultimate response to those who would see historic preservation as mere sentiment. In this book we see the functional worth, the economic value, the sheer common sense of historic preservation. This is an album of the best efforts to preserve and reuse older buildings, and through them to make our cities, in the very best sense, civilized places. *Remaking America* is not only a book of celebration, but should also spur the movement onward.

FOREWORD

BY DR. JOHN BRADEMAS

In 1978, when I wrote a preface to Barbaralee Diamonstein's first book on the adaptive reuse of buildings, the concept of historic preservation was still novel.

Now, nearly a decade later, the preservation movement is flourishing. Its vitality is evident in scores of revived Main Streets, in $2.2 billion of rehabilitation generated annually through federal tax incentives, in more than a thousand locally designated historic districts, and in over 250,000 buildings listed in the National Register of Historic Places.

Two words from the title of Dr. Diamonstein's earlier book, *Buildings Reborn*, catch the redemptive quality associated with a religious commitment and translate that quality into an attitude that she believes crucial to what we do, or fail to do, about our built environment. For the sites and structures of earlier times are incarnations, often irreplaceable, of the American heritage. They teach us of our traditions. They embody the continuity of our culture.

When we thoughtlessly obliterate the buildings and places of our past, we demonstrate an insensitivity to what we were, a disdain for what we in part still are. By saving—and adapting for reuse—the best of our buildings, we link the communities of today to the foundations of our culture.

As our towns and cities grow and our commercial, industrial, and residential areas expand, the task of safeguarding our national legacy becomes more difficult. We often meet the demands for more living and working space by tearing down existing structures, frequently erecting new ones at the same location. But in responding to the requirements of the present and future, we need not always destroy the old. Wise preservation can renew the integrity and utility of a structure and reestablish a place for it in the life of a community.

Examples of this regenerative process are many and multiplying. Among those in this book are the $135 million renovation of the St. Louis Union Station, one of the country's largest adaptive reuse projects. This huge structure, built in 1894, will become a hotel, indoor park, and constellation of shops and restaurants. On a much smaller scale, the Jayne House of Philadelphia, a splendid example of Victorian architecture, now houses a suite of law offices.

The imaginative recycling of commercial properties is illustrated by two other projects. The executive headquarters for Sears, Roebuck & Co., in Washington, D.C., is located in what used to be three separate landmark commercial buildings. In San Francisco, a former warehouse has been transformed into the new Giftcenter, with 160 showrooms and display facilities for the wholesale gift market.

As a member of Congress for twenty-two years (1959–1981), I must note that the interest of the federal government in protecting and preserving places of historic importance reaches back to the start of the century, a considerable time in the life of a nation so young. The Antiquities Act of 1906 authorized the president to proclaim as national monuments buildings and landmarks on federal property. With the creation of the National Park Service in 1916, the secretary of the interior was authorized to provide for the preservation and restoration of historic properties of national significance.

A generation later, in 1949, Congress chartered the National Trust for Historic Preservation, a nongovernmental organization devoted to the preservation of such properties, both public and private.

After nearly two decades more, Congress in 1966 approved the National Historic Preservation Act (NHPA), major legislation that expanded the federal commitment in this area. The law grew from the recommendations of a study group organized by the United States Conference of Mayors, whose findings had been published as a book, *With Heritage So Rich.*

NHPA has been the foundation of historic preservation in the United States for almost twenty years. The law established the National Advisory Council on Historic Preservation to encourage a more vigorous national program for saving our heritage of structures and sites. The legislation requires the secretary of the interior to maintain a register of historic properties and provides federal matching grants to the states to assist in their preservation efforts.

Not until 1976, however, was there a change in federal policy that would significantly enhance historic preservation in this country. That year, with the Tax Reform Act of 1976, Congress for the first time provided tax incentives for rehabilitation projects. Major revisions were made in these incentives with passage of the Economic Recovery Tax Act of 1981 and in subsequent amendments to the tax laws.

The Internal Revenue Code now provides a three-tiered system of investment tax credits for the cost of rehabilitating buildings. A 25 percent investment tax credit is available for the rehabilitation of a structure listed in the National Register of Historic Places or located within a certified historical district. Renovation of other structures may qualify for a 20 percent tax credit if a building is at least forty years old and a 15 percent credit if at least thirty.

The 25 percent historic tax credit alone has since 1981 generated $5 billion of private investment in more than 6,800 buildings. And this tax incentive has had a major impact on local economies, bringing stimulus, in particular, to older, declining neighborhoods. Since 1982, the credit has generated more than $5.3 billion in sales and business activity, provided a $4 billion increase in wages, and put an estimated 180,500 people to work.

Despite the success of these various measures, there has been a continuing struggle in recent years over federal preservation policy. To the extent that the rehabilitation of buildings depends on support from the national Administration, the preservation movement has felt beleaguered since Ronald Reagan took office.

Although in Mr. Reagan's first term his Administration did support rehabilitation tax credits, it relied on these incentives to the exclusion of all else. Since fiscal 1982, the Administration's annual budget proposal has contained no funds at all for state preservation programs, and since 1983, no money for the National Trust for Historic Preservation. And the budget request for fiscal 1985 cut funds for the Advisory Council on Historic Preservation by a third.

In his budget for fiscal 1986, Mr. Reagan continued on this destructive course. Moreover, in the so-called tax-reform plan he proposed in 1985, the president sought to abolish the preservation tax credits.

Mr. Reagan's actions have, unhappily, not matched his rhetoric. For in the spring of 1985, the president declared that the preservation credits had "fostered a revival of skilled craftsmanship, introduced unusual job opportunities in a changing economy, and brought about a philosophical change by demonstrating that the old buildings of America can be as serviceable, economical, and important as the new."

With federal laws to encourage preservation under attack, the appearance of Barbaralee Diamonstein's new book could not be more propitious. Dr. Diamonstein, moreover, is splendidly qualified to write such a study. Her interests, experience, and education are extraordinarily diverse, encompassing the arts, politics, journalism, and social reform, and her illuminating analysis reflects her range of concerns.

Remaking America will, I am confident, inspire many citizens to adapt the best in the sites and structures of our past to the service of people today and tomorrow. And the book will, we can hope, help move the leaders of our national government to support a federal policy that will protect rather than abandon the heritage of American architecture.

INTRODUCTION

BY BARBARALEE DIAMONSTEIN

When I began my research on *Buildings Reborn: New Uses, Old Places*, the adaptive reuse phenomenon was growing apace as ever-increasing numbers of American communities looked for ways to preserve our architectural and cultural heritage. But the concept was still new enough for many to argue that it was merely a passing fad. After all, how many chocolate factories were available for conversion into Ghirardelli Squares, and how many crumbling produce sheds could be reincarnated as Quincy Markets? That was 1976. Now, a decade later, it is clear that the historic preservation movement and, within it, the phenomenon of adaptive reuse, have not subsided, but have, in fact, continued to gather force. The insistence on preserving our past, on recycling, rather than razing our built environment, is with us to stay.

Scarcely a major city in the United States has not been touched, and in some cases almost completely transformed, by the preservation movement. In countless smaller cities and towns and villages as well, the impulse to save the gabled old house on Main Street from deterioration or the Beaux-Arts railroad terminal from the wrecker's ball is manifest. The point of the effort is nothing less than to preserve our past, to provide an anchor for our collective memory.

Preservation does not, and emphatically should not, mean merely restoration. Otherwise, the entire movement would have added little more than a few extra stops on the Wednesday house tour, a few more Williamsburgs, a few additional museums. Probably the single most important aspect of the preservation movement is recycling—adapting old buildings to uses different from the ones for which they were originally intended. This phenomenon goes under myriad names, not all of them entirely apt: renovation, rehabilitation, remodeling, recycling, retrofitting, environmental retrieval, extended use, and, possibly most precise of all, adaptive reuse. By whatever name, it has made available to the smallest town and the most modest commercial enterprise a practical means of preservation.

Perhaps nothing has done more to make recycling economically attractive than two little-known pieces of legislation: a provision of the 1976 Tax Reform Act permitting faster tax write-offs for restoration (or recycling) of properties of historical value; and a section of the 1981 Economic Recovery Tax Act permitting tax deduction of up to 25 percent of the value of such work. It did not take builders long to realize that these new features made economic as well as architectural sense. From 1977 to 1981, projects involving a total of $1.1 billion in construction qualified for the tax breaks. That sum was matched in 1982 alone, when another $1.1 billion in projects were also approved. A year later, in 1983, that figure had *doubled*, to $2.2 billion. Nor does the pace appear to have slowed significantly; in 1984, the figure was $2.1 billion. That represented some 2,100 projects, and according to J. Jackson Walter, president of the National Trust for Historic Preservation, "two-thirds of these wouldn't have happened without the incentives. The buildings would have been torn down or allowed to decay. More of America's architectural and cultural heritage would have been lost."

This upsurge in recycling activity made my task all the easier. Although I had combed the United States only a decade ago for what I thought were ninety-five particularly interesting examples of buildings that had been kept alive by consciously changing their roles, I had no difficulty finding forty-eight fresh examples when I set out once again. In fact, the major challenge was in winnowing the possibilities down to merely forty-eight.

I began by writing thousands of letters to city officials, historic societies, landmarks commissions, architects, preservationists, and citizens across the country, requesting information, recommendations, and referrals about adaptive reuse projects. The response was overwhelming; every town and city, it seems, has a special "reborn building" that it thought should be considered. Of the thousands proposed, I seriously considered several hundred whose new functions and design changes not only are consonant with the original architecture and modern surroundings, but also enhance both. Then began the elaborate process of documenting the buildings: accumulating historical information, architectural description, before-and-after photographs, and fresh anecdotal materials. Endless research ensued, including interviews, conversations, and digging in archives.

This book attempts to give a representative, rather than definitive, assessment of the range of projects that have been or are being undertaken across the United States. I have tried to cover the spectrum from the idiosyncratic (the Old Carroll County Jail, Carrollton, Kentucky) to the monumental (Sundance Square, Fort Worth, Texas). Because of constraints of space, deadlines, and availability of materials, quite a few worthy projects had to be excluded. But among the forty-eight that were chosen, I have tried to reflect geographic diversity (West Coast as well as East,

small towns and large cities) as well as a diversity of building types (places to work and to shop, to play and to live).

As for photographs, they were contributed by the architects, designers, developers, or property owners, or by the photographers themselves. Some are "homemade," taken by a local enthusiast. Some were produced by the best architectural photographers in the country. In some projects, the "before"—prior to renovation—photographs are very old and therefore difficult to reproduce clearly. They have been included to illustrate the building's history and relevance. On one level, the building may have historical significance, and on another it may have community significance in that it is an important part of the economic or cultural development of its surroundings. In some projects, "after" photographs do not exist of buildings that were still under construction as this book went to print; in those cases, drawings and renderings of the proposed structures are included.

I deliberately limited my selections to the United States, although there is certainly no shortage of candidates abroad. Europe, particularly, possesses a sense of what Yale art historian Vincent Scully calls "urban architecture as representing communication across generations over time." Rome may well be the supreme example of a city where the ongoing process of renewal by conversion has succeeded. The Parisian art critic Pierre Schneider describes the aptly named Eternal City as "the scene of a permanent and ubiquitous process of architectural and urbanistic readjustments, adjunctions, subtractions which, causing the despair of the archaeological purists, have been the prime factor in keeping the city present, in endowing it with a magic one never encounters in the mummified historical monument." Many of the great cities of Europe were nearly destroyed during World War II, yet when the time came to rebuild, there was seldom thought of starting from scratch. Instead, the historic cores of London, Warsaw, Prague, and Leningrad were restored or rebuilt pretty much as they had been.

In the United States, the first official recognition that even in a country so "new" there were things worth saving did not come until the early days of this century, with the Antiquities Act of 1906. In 1916, the National Park Service was created, essentially to preserve prehistoric sites and artifacts of the West. At the same time, Congress proclaimed a national policy (though not a national practice, unfortunately) of preserving for public use historic sites, buildings, and objects of national significance. In 1949, Congress established the private not-for-profit National Trust for Historic Preservation. Ten years after its formation, its members numbered around 4,500. In 1978, that number had skyrocketed to 125,000, and in 1985, the trust claimed a membership of more than 160,000. More important, perhaps, it can count on many times that number for support. As Michael Pittas, architect, planner, and former director of the Design Arts Program of the National Endowment for the Arts, put it, "Concern with preservation is no longer restricted to the enlightened, well-educated people who you would expect to see standing before city councils and boards of estimate and fighting the good fight." Just about everyone everywhere is in on the action. Listen to Prince Charles of England: "At last people are

beginning to realize that it is possible, and important in human terms, to respect old buildings, street plans, and traditional scales. At last, after witnessing the wholesale destruction of Georgian and Victorian housing in most cities, people have begun to realize that it *is* possible to restore old buildings." Or President Ronald Reagan: "The old buildings of America can be as serviceable, economical, and important as the new." Or the Supreme Court of the United States, in a 1978 opinion: "Structures with special historic, cultural, or architectural significance enhance the quality of life for all. Historic conservation is but one aspect of the much larger problem . . . of enhancing—or perhaps developing for the first time—the quality of life for people."

As recently as 1965, only one hundred cities across the United States had established landmarks preservation commissions. A decade later, the number had increased fivefold. Today, it stands at approximately one thousand. Private redevelopment has increased, but builders still must win approval for their plans from these commissions. Such commissions, and the work they have approved, have meant a great deal to many American communities. Discussing the 25 percent tax credit for rehabilitating buildings at least fifty years old, J. Jackson Walter has noted: "The mayors of Chicago, Providence, Boston, Philadelphia, Savannah, and Dallas admitted, even strenuously boasted, that historic preservation was a cornerstone for future prosperity for their cities."

In a relatively short time span, adaptive reuse has clearly become imbedded in the American consciousness and its physical character as well. What was it that set off the recycling movement, one that is remaking America both economically and aesthetically? What helped provide the impetus to make it such a significant feature of American daily life? Four factors have been at work—architectural, attitudinal, economic, and demographic.

The decline of modernism

In 1977, architecture critic Charles Jencks proclaimed that modern architecture had "expired finally and completely." Many critics shared his conviction, at least to a degree. John Morris Dixon, in a discussion of some of the changes that had taken place in his twenty-five years as editor of *Progressive Architecture*, noted that in 1960 the prevailing wisdom was the modernists' rigid insistence on purity, which ruled out not merely ornamentation but historical allusion and almost any sort of complexity as well. Now, wrote Dixon, "we can look upon the whole body of historical architecture as worthy of examination and interpretation." Modernism's pure functionalism decreed that once something had outlived its purpose, it had to be destroyed, to give way to new structures suitable to new functions. To create an architecture purified and liberated from the past, modernism demanded that the historical architectural symbols identified with the old be swept away.

It did not take long for modernism's successor, however, to run into heavy weather, partly because of the same sort of unyielding orthodoxy. As Chicago architect Helmut Jahn explains: "Just as Modernism refuses to acknowledge anything which had to do with history, Post-Modernism refuses to acknowledge anything which has to do with Modernism." Paul Goldberger, Pulitzer Prize–winning architecture critic of the *New York Times*, agreed: "The more ornate creations of postmodernism have begun to feel heavy-handed and not a little graceless," he wrote in 1985. "At least part of the current benign view of modernism must come out of reaction to certain postmodern works that now seem overbearing and forced. This hardly means that we are moving away from postmodernism. We will continue to see more and more buildings that rely heavily on historical form, for the rejection of history which was so central to modernism's ideology is hardly going to return to us."

Recognizing the limitations of both modernism and postmodernism, we may now be embarking on a new era in American architecture (post-postmodernism, perhaps?) characterized by a kind of calculated diversity. Eclecticism and individualism are invalidating the dominance of any single design ideology. As the distinguished architect Robert Venturi has said, "There is an accompanying desire of people to understand their own particular heritage, their own unique qualities, and acknowledge them. This is a time for eclecticism over neoclassicism, for employing many kinds of symbolism and formal systems in architecture."

The growing allure of the old

For much of America's history, new meant good, newer meant better. Now, in a veritable revolution in American attitudes, we are seeing a reversal of what Walt Whitman called "the pull-down-and-build-over-again spirit" of the United States. Change meant progress, progress meant newness, and newness meant throwing out the old—including the built world. The pioneer ethos and the frontier had much to do with this. Out West, a Main Street would be built between breakfast and dinner and a whole town would sprout overnight at the sites of the great gold and silver and copper strikes, and what went up in practically no time often came down just as quickly.

Adaptive reuse exemplifies this new shift in attitude. As the New York City Landmarks Preservation Commission said more than ten years ago, "Creative adaption provides pride in our heritage, a link with the past, respect for the aesthetics and craftsmanship of another time, insights into our own development, ample creative opportunity for architectural innovation and problem solving, enhancement of the urban fabric, greater security, stability and beauty, while conserving basic materials and meeting modern needs." To some extent, adaptive reuse is an extension of common sense to architecture, a pragmatic realization that it is practically impossible to remain purist about the functions of a building. It permits us to live in converted schools, to shop in converted post offices, to study in converted train stations. In a sense, recycling can also be seen as a form of architectural criticism. Writer Norman Mailer was thinking of this when he proposed "Mailer's Law of Precedence" (pronounced pree-*cee*-dence): "If the building across the street looks better than the building that you're in, then the building across the street was built earlier."

There is no guarantee, however, that old buildings, even those worth preserving, will actu-

ally be preserved. Benjamin Thompson, whose recycling projects include Boston's Faneuil Hall–Quincy Market complex and New York's South Street Seaport, stated: "Most old buildings are eminently worth saving because they speak to us about time and tradition and where we came from, and because they display materials and workmanship that we cannot afford to duplicate today. . . . [However,] without an attempt to use some imagination in both preserving and updating them, most of our heritage buildings [are] going to be disposed of." In other words, if the worthwhile buildings are to be saved, they will have to be saved for something other than mere restoration—or mummification, as some critics put it.

Economic factors

In the 1970s, recession brought bulldozers to a virtual halt. Construction was one of the country's hardest-hit industries. With dwindling opportunities to demolish and then build from scratch, adaptive reuse emerged as a logical solution. It was cheaper and more labor-intensive than new construction, with every $1 million generating 107 jobs for a retrofitting versus 68 for a new building. Today the economic climate is far different, and many cities are in the midst of the greatest building boom since the 1960s. The area between 34th and 60th streets and between Third and Eighth avenues in Manhattan, for example, saw 142 high-rise buildings go up between 1960 and 1979, or some seven and a half a year. In the three years between 1979 and 1982, a total of thirty high-rises were begun or completed in the same area, or ten a year. This represents a 25 percent increase in the rate of building, quite significant when one considers the dwindling number of developable sites in what is perhaps the most densely overbuilt area in the world. Throughout the country, other cities such as Dallas and Pittsburgh have experienced similar booms.

Yet in spite of the fact that we can now more readily afford to build new structures, we are still channeling enormous effort and funds into recycling old ones. A major reason for this has been two important tax breaks for restoring and recycling in the last decade. In 1976, the federal government started a tax incentive program for historic preservation. The 1981 Economic Recovery Tax Act allows newly renovated buildings at least thirty years old to qualify for a 15 percent tax investment credit, those at least forty years old to qualify for 20 percent. To qualify for 25 percent, buildings must meet two requirements: the money spent on rehabilitation must exceed the adjusted basis of the building (which is defined as the cost of the building plus capital improvements, minus the value of the land and depreciation) or $5,000 in a two-year period; and 75 percent of the external walls must remain intact after the renovation. These tax investment credits are especially appealing to builders because they are dollar-for-dollar tax savings, deductible from actual taxes owed rather than from gross income. Owners are further helped by the Accelerated Cost Recovery System, which allows them to depreciate acquisition and rehabilitation costs over a fifteen-year period.

Speaking recently of the benefits that the recycling movement derived from the 1981 tax act, President Reagan noted: "Our tax incentives have made the preservation of our older buildings not only a matter of respect for beauty and history,

but also of economic good sense." During the last five years, however, Reagan has significantly reduced allocations for the Historic Preservation Fund, from $42.2 million in 1980 ($37 million to the states and $5.2 million to the National Trust for Historic Preservation) to $25.48 million for fiscal year 1986 ($21.07 million to the states and $4.41 million to the trust). Because of these cuts, private investment becomes increasingly important. Loans and grants from the trust have been generating an average of $9 to every $1 from the trust, which could help pick up the slack.

Demographic changes

Much of the upsurge in recycling has been concentrated in the nation's cities. Today's new breed of city dwellers do not view urban living as a mere stepping-stone to the greener pastures of suburbia, but as a long-term goal in and of itself. The suburban house, the 1950s symbol of stability, respectability, and success, has been replaced, accordingly, by the urban cooperative or condominium. In many cities, rental property— long the embodiment of transient urban living—is rapidly becoming a phenomenon of the past, and many of the amenities long associated with suburban living are now present in the urban environment. In many instances, co-op or condo buyers purchase places with a garage, a health club, an atrium, even an in-house grocery or beauty shop.

The desire to return to the city has been fueled by the increased number of women in the work force. It would take powerful pastoral urges to persuade a two-career couple (52 percent of Americans) to live in the suburbs if that meant both would have to commute. In families with children, if both parents work it is often thought to be preferable that they both work near home. In any event, the temporal, spatial, economic, and emotional constraints of modern city living have resulted in smaller families—and, in fact, some two-career couples are deciding not to have children at all.

As a result of changing demographic and family patterns, some primary institutions, such as schools and churches, are dwindling in number. Those forced to close their doors become prime targets for adaptive reuse, as did the thousands of abandoned railroad terminals and powerhouses that dot the American landscape.

Historically, cities have been centers for both trading and manufacturing. Today, because of the increasing demand for urban housing, center city property values have skyrocketed. Often it is neither economically feasible nor technologically suitable for manufacturers to maintain their center city locations, prompting many firms to move to the suburbs or other regions of the country. In the Northeast, the economies of the new urban centers focus on service and high-tech industries. Often the new urban dweller is employed—and paid well—by these industries.

Cyclical changes in the economy are mirrored in the real estate market. The recent economic upswing has affected neighborhood usage patterns in the cities; people are living and working in the cities, but they are also shopping and playing in them. As the cities become more commonly used, or, more appropriately, reused, as places to live, the problem of space becomes more critical. In many cases, the only neighborhoods that can accommodate the new urban-

ites are those that were formerly considered marginal or depressed. Sometimes old or abandoned structures in these areas are razed to make way for larger housing complexes. Other times, there are obsolete structures that can be converted, added to, and renewed. In most cases there is a choice: replace or recycle.

Boston architect Graham Gund hints at an answer when he says: "A city should be a mix of old and new; the new should be used to stitch together the old, to create spaces that bring people together." There is much to be gained if we can create an urban fabric that repairs the crumbling past while blending it with the present. There is also much to be gained from the interaction of old and new residents in these neighborhoods.

The long-term residents tend to be the less affluent or even poor, the elderly, or minorities. The newly arrived tend to be economically privileged and firmly middle-class in their attitudes and aspirations. Can it work? Can old be stitched with new? Will the new simply push out the old, and re-create the gentrified enclaves for the middle class that long characterized the suburbs? Unfortunately, many long-term residents and small shopkeepers *are* being displaced, but some legislative remedies are belatedly being concocted. "Sweat equity" programs allow local/original residents to gentrify without the gentry. Rather than standing by while outside forces displace them either by razing or retrofitting neighborhood buildings, the locals are, in a growing number of cases, restoring, recycling, and continuing to use the buildings themselves. The National Trust for Historic Preservation and the New York Landmarks Conservancy, in a joint effort pioneered by the

National Trust, have established an Inner Cities Ventures Fund in New York, whose purpose is to help find funds "for the rehabilitation of landmark quality and designated historic buildings in low and moderate income neighborhoods in New York City by not-for-profit community groups."

For all its positive results, the adaptive reuse phenomenon has not escaped criticism. Philosophical and economic complaints, as well as questions of appropriate design, are being raised by preservationists, developers, and neighborhood residents alike. One of the loudest outcries—one that would never have been raised but for the flourishing success of adaptive reuse—is that traditional rehabilitation concerns, such as historical and architectural integrity, are being overshadowed by the commercial interests of private developers. Ada Louise Huxtable, former *New York Times* architecture critic, pointed to the South Street Seaport, a commercial fishing center converted into a fashionable mall along New York City's East River, as a potential example of this controversy. "The city is about to sacrifice the last of the genuine character of a fragile historical survival to economic development masquerading as a way to save the past," she wrote. "Out of innocence, or ignorance, we continue to make the kinds of bargains for preservation that turn out not to be bargains at all." Huxtable identified a growing concern. Too often preservation is coming to be equated with the construction of vast commercial malls, and one cannot help but wonder if this is a fad of which the public will soon tire. These "merchandising shrines" or "cathedrals of consumption" may eviscerate the original architecture and its history, leaving a much slicker and more controlled atmosphere. The worry is not a new one. In 1896, Louis Sullivan warned that the architect's function must be to rectify: "Otherwise," wrote Sullivan, "architecture, as a fine art, goes to the bargain counter, and the people become merely shoppers; and so through bargain and sale, values must tend ever downward and the buyers become ever more sordid."

Issues such as those posed by commercial malls impress upon us the need for an intelligent, educated, overall policy of adaptive reuse. The phenomenon has matured enough so that our attention now must not simply focus on "saving" buildings or neighborhoods but encompass more complicated considerations. What criteria should be applied, for example, in determining which structures to rehabilitate? Some buildings may have qualities completely apart from architectural detail that mark them as worthy of saving and reusing. A structure may have special significance within a community, as in the case of one old building in Watts, an inner-city area of Los Angeles, that was a factory during the Depression and at that time employed the parents of many current residents. The structure was preserved and converted into a shopping plaza not because of its high architectural distinction but because it is, to the community, a place of genuine meaning. The same was true of Dubrow's, a legendary cafeteria (now demolished) in New York City's garment district that for decades served as a special meeting place for the neighborhood's older male workers. Though not legally designated a landmark, it had unofficially been awarded that title for its unique contribution to the community.

A building is much more than an architectural

or engineering accomplishment—it is the reflection of a community's history and personality. Thus, reasons for recycling buildings, for preserving areas, must sometimes reach beyond the purely architectural. William Conklin, himself an architect and former vice-chairman of the New York City Landmarks Preservation Commission, put it one way. "Buildings," he said in an interview, "are like friends. Just as we respect the structure of our social relationships in the world, so we should value our urban context. When we wipe out our buildings, we wipe out not just the physical objects but many more subtle urban networks." The late José Luis Sert, dean of the Harvard Graduate School of Design, put it more succinctly when he argued in 1966 that Boston's Commonwealth Avenue should be preserved because "it is lively. Although the architecture is not great, it has character and harmony."

As the preservation and adaptive reuse movements mature, we seem to be outgrowing the compulsion to freeze in amber every colonial salt-box or Victorian mansion. There are, after all, some seventeen million buildings in the United States that are at least fifty years old, and not even a zealot would want all of these preserved, or even a large fraction of them. We also seem to be developing broader interests concerning what should be preserved, as is evidenced by the growing fascination with industrial architecture. Because we long viewed industrialization as a major factor in the demolition of our physical heritage, we refused to acknowledge its structures as potentially recyclable. Today we consider the remnants of America's industrial era,

the furnaces and foundries and mills of our "Gilded Age," also worthy of reuse. The Sloss Furnaces in Birmingham, Alabama, are a prime example. These structures, squat, muscular, and plug-ugly, have absolutely nothing of the charm of an antebellum plantation house, but are they not of historical significance that may even surpass the mansion's? If rehabilitating industrial architecture makes perfectly good sense to us today, however, that was not the case twenty or so years ago, at the outset of the contemporary preservation movement. But back then, who would have guessed that we would someday seek to preserve New York's Lever House (Park Avenue's first glass skyscraper), or the Gropius House in Lincoln, Massachusetts, or the first drive-in restaurant, the McDonald's in Des Plaines, Illinois? And perhaps these too will be recycled one day.

Just as we have refined our ideas on *what* should be recycled, so have we developed more sophisticated theories about *how* we should recycle. More and more, for example, projects involving adaptive reuse find themselves intertwined with the complicated architectural issue of contextualism. This is because adaptive reuse requires harmony of old and new, where strict restoration does not. In demanding good modern design as well as respect for what already exists, adaptive reuse is unique.

Contextualism pushes the concept of harmony beyond individual buildings to include entire blocks and neighborhoods. While the success of an adaptive reuse project depends largely on how compatible the new use is to the old building, compatibility within the surrounding environmental context is also important. As William Conklin recently said: "A building should relate to its existing context and be respectful of that context. It should not make the adjacent buildings look ridiculous; it should not cast the other buildings in its shadow. But it should make a positive contribution, not only by its function, but by being something special on the street." Paul Goldberger makes the point that the concern with contextualism became possible only when the iron sway of modernism ended. "Modernism was concerned with the creation of a pure and perfect object," he wrote. "Architecture today shifts its priorities to the making of buildings that relate to their physical context, that fulfill users' needs and that relate to cultural context as well."

The key to the success of adaptive reuse is recognizing those buildings or streets that are, or once were, special, whether for architectural, historical, or cultural reasons. These are the structures we must struggle to retain. We have already seen that perhaps the most creative and economical means of saving them is adaptive reuse. Some idealistic preservationists may argue that ultimately nothing is superior to maintaining the original building, as well as its function. The late scholar Walter Muir Whitehill was not one of them. In 1966, twenty years ago, in a prophetic report produced by a special committee on historic preservation titled *With Heritage So Rich*, Whitehill wrote: "We already have on exhibition more historic houses and museums than we need or are good for us as a nation. Indeed, they multiply so

fast that some form of institutional contraception must soon be invented. . . . Let us save what we have around us that is good, not for exhibition, not for 'education,' but for practical use as places to live in and to work in. Preservationists should try to keep America beautiful, rather than to create little paradises of nostalgia in an ocean of superhighways and loudspeakers, billboards, neon signs, parking lots, used-car dumps and hot-dog stands." That advice will be more pertinent than ever as we move into the 1990s and the realities of a rapidly changing world demand that we develop ever more culturally and technologically appropriate uses for our old structures.

In the end, the issue of adaptive reuse pivots on the most fundamental of conflicts: age versus youth, the old versus the new. Neither has a corner on virtue. As Paul Goldberger writes: "Preservationists are guilty far too often of indiscriminately insisting that old automatically means good. . . . On the other hand . . . architects have too often given them sufficient reason to believe the converse—that new must mean bad. That isn't true either and the preservation movement cannot go on acting as if it were so."

Architect William Pedersen puts it another way: "To reconcile the old and the new, one must bring a respect and an understanding of both, and then search for an architectural strategy that fuses these two polarities. . . . Architecture that excludes one or the other is profoundly pessimistic."

By fusing past and present, adaptive reuse is an inherently optimistic process. Here are forty-eight examples to prove it.

NORTH

CHESAPEAKE COMMONS
BALTIMORE, MARYLAND

FROM: High school
TO: Rental apartments

In the early years of the nineteenth century, the burgeoning port city of Baltimore felt a responsibility to expand its free public school system to accommodate the growing numbers of residents drawn by the flourishing shipping industry. Although this attention was limited at that time to the education of white males, it was nevertheless a pioneering venture. In 1839, the Baltimore City College, a public high school, was founded—the third-oldest high school in the country. After several moves, it settled at what is now City Hall Plaza in 1843. A new City College building was completed in 1875, but that building was condemned in 1892 because the construction of a tunnel weakened the building's foundation. Immediately afterward, in 1893, the Baltimore School Board called for a new building to "increase the number of class rooms, and to furnish more light and ventilation, and other facilities which are essential for the future success of the college." The commission for this task was given to the firm of Baldwin and Pennington, Baltimore's premier architects of the late nineteenth century. The firm designed many of Baltimore's more significant buildings, including the Maryland Club, the Fidelity Building, the Mount Royal Station, the Camden Station, and part of the Pier Four Power Plant.

The new City College building was designed to be harmonious with those of Johns Hopkins University just down the road, also designed by Baldwin and Pennington. The plan oriented the building toward a small plaza, facing the university. Its design was a combination of two architectural styles: Romanesque Revival and Beaux-Arts classicism. The six-story central facade is flanked by square towers at the corners. Among the distinctive features of the design were three-story-high arches, a projecting classical portico, ornately decorated cornices, bands of garland decorations and lion's heads, Spanish tile roofs, balconies on the fifth-floor towers, and large brick pilasters topped with Ionic capitals. In sheer size and degree of ornamentation, City College overwhelmed every existing public school in Baltimore.

Shortly after the building opened in 1899, there was a sharp increase in attendance at the school. From thirty-six students in 1900, the size of the graduating class alone exceeded four hundred by 1926. The assembly hall, attic, and basement were converted to classroom use, and students were forced to attend school in shifts. By 1928, Baltimore City College was forced to move to larger quarters, but the building kept that name, carved in limestone over the entrance.

Between 1928 and 1978, the building served a number of educational institutions, including a vocational school, a high school, and a community college. After the college closed in 1978, the building was left vacant, and allowed to deteriorate.

In 1980, a blazing fire gutted the old City College building. The roof was destroyed, and all that remained of the interior was some charred walls. Burned and abandoned, the building stood dormant for two years before the Schneider Group of Ann Arbor, Michigan, a development and design firm, saw the potential for rehabilitation and purchased the property. Working with the local Market Center Development

ABOVE: *Elevation, after.* Baltimore's foremost architectural firm of the era, Baldwin and Pennington, designed the school to harmonize with its earlier buildings at nearby Johns Hopkins University.

BELOW: *Exterior, after.* Chesapeake Commons is located between Seton Hill and Mount Vernon; the project helps form a stable, safe residential zone, to link two historic Baltimore neighborhoods.

RIGHT: *The 1980 fire.* A blazing fire gutted the old City College building. The roof was destroyed, and the fire left only charred walls in the interior.

FAR RIGHT: *Exterior, before.* Built in the 1890s for Baltimore City College, a public high school, and later used by other educational institutions, the vacant building was gutted by fire in 1980.

BELOW: *Exterior, after.* Other facilities include a communal courtyard and a gatehouse, as well as an entertainment and exercise center.

Corporation, the firm spent $11 million to adapt the structure to quality residential use. The building and site have been renamed Chesapeake Commons. On an adjoining site, the developers are renovating a row of townhouses on Academy Alley, a small thoroughfare along the side of Chesapeake Commons. That project will feature shops, offices, and a pedestrian mews and will form a more pleasant approach and entrance to the larger structure.

While it was fortunate that the exterior of Chesapeake Commons remained relatively unscathed by the fire, the interior had to be completely rehabilitated. Under the direction of Estelle Schneider, the developer and design supervisor, the original six-story structure has been converted into ninety-eight multilevel units of one and two bedrooms. Every apartment has a unique floor plan; some feature rooftop terraces, private gardens, and spiral staircases. The rough texture of exposed brick walls has been highlighted in many rooms, and some triplex layouts have 42-foot-high ceilings. Common facilities for residents include a courtyard and gatehouse and an entertainment and exercise center.

Chesapeake Commons is located in Market Center, a traditional retail district flanked on either side by two historic neighborhoods, Seton Hill and Mount Vernon. It was long considered crucial that a new residential zone be built in Market Center, to form a more stable, safe link between the neighborhoods. In helping to arrange financing for the project, the Market Center Development Corporation, along with local residents, hopes that Chesapeake Commons will prove a catalyst for the renewal of the entire neighborhood.

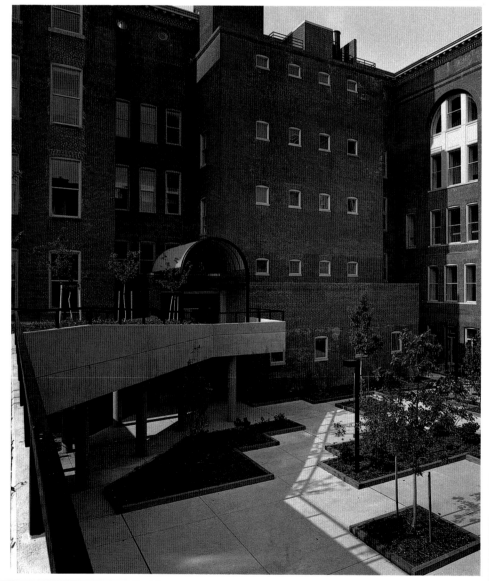

ABOVE: *Interior, after.* Under the direction of Estelle Schneider, the developer and design supervisor, the original six-story structure was converted into ninety-eight multilevel one- and two-bedroom units.

RIGHT: *Interior, after.* Each of the ninety-eight one- or two-bedroom apartments is unique. Some triplex apartments have 42-foot-high ceilings.

THE ROCKINGHAM CANAL HOUSE
B E L L O W S   F A L L S ,   V E R M O N T

FROM: Hotel
TO: Housing and retail space

The Rockingham Canal House, built in 1883, is located in the historic central business district of the village of Bellows Falls, Vermont. Its development into senior citizen housing, completed nearly one hundred years later, was the focus of a community-initiated drive for economic revitalization. Early on, residents decided that the restructuring of the town's faltering economy would rely on the preservation of its cultural heritage.

The village of Bellows Falls was founded in 1752, at the 52-foot-high Great Falls of the Connecticut River. Through the mid-nineteenth century the village served as a transportation crossroads: the Bellows Falls Canal was completed in 1802 (the first navigation canal built in the United States), and passage up the river beyond the falls was at last possible. In the mid-1880s the canal's nine locks were removed. Once it no longer served its navigational function, the canal became a sluiceway to provide water power and to drive electric generators. At the same time, Bellows Falls had become one of the most important railroad junctions in northern New England. Toward the end of the nineteenth century, the village's railroad transport and available energy led to the growth of industry in the area, primarily paper mills and machinery manufacturers.

At approximately the same time, the Bellows Falls central business district took on its present Victorian style. The original Rockingham Hotel was built by Leverett T. Lovell II, on a site chosen for its accessibility to the railroad station across the street. Lovell's name and the construction date were engraved on the many-colored scalloped slate shingles on two sides of the building's mansard roof. Harry Houdini was among the actors and performers who appeared at the Opera House, located on the same block, and who often stayed at the Rockingham Hotel. The trains provided most of the hotel's patrons, who enjoyed its hospitality and fine food; the vegetables served in its restaurant were grown on the proprietor's own farm. The hotel was a central presence in the town, as a hub of activity, as the largest and most architecturally significant structure, and as an attraction for residents in the surrounding rural area.

Just before the 1929 Depression, Bellows Falls' economic fortunes began their own decline, and the physical character of the village followed suit. By 1937 a rectangular brick movie theater was constructed at the rear of the Rockingham Hotel, obstructing part of the arcaded south facade. The hotel was subsequently used as a rooming house and bar, until it was closed by the state fire marshal's office in 1960.

The building remained unused, and deteriorating, until the early 1970s, when the community-established Townscape Improvement Committee planned for its renovation. With the Vermont Division of Historic Preservation, the committee sponsored a study to identify improvements needed in Bellows Falls, and in 1976 it formed a nonprofit downtown development corporation to purchase and develop the hotel site. Revenue-sharing funds were used to make the purchase and for emergency repairs on the building. The village held a design/development competition for proposals that would work financially, be an asset to the village, and save the historic Rockingham Hotel. A proposal to create forty-two units of hous-

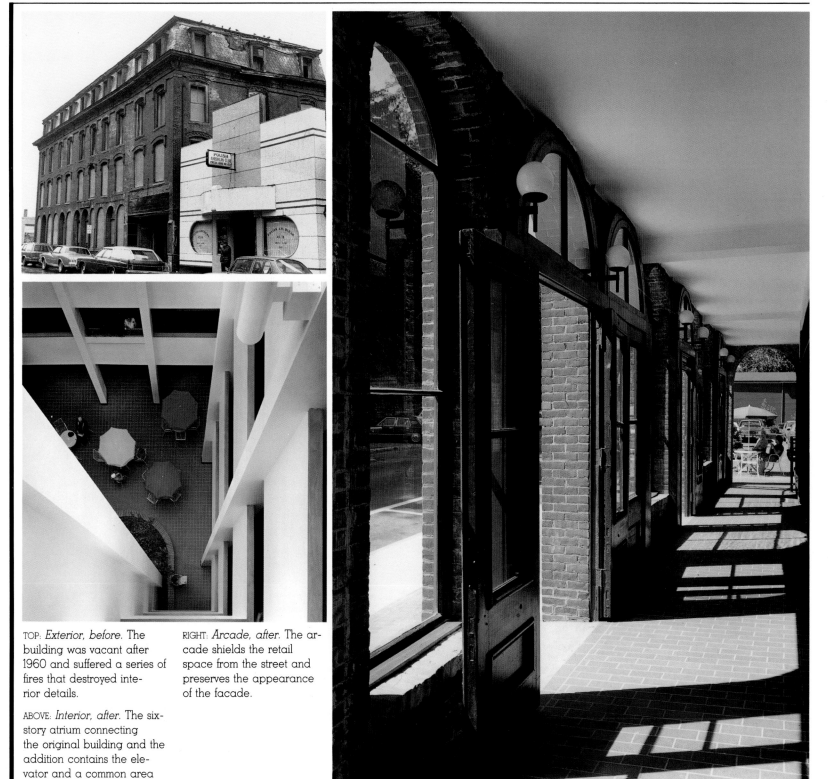

TOP: *Exterior, before.* The building was vacant after 1960 and suffered a series of fires that destroyed interior details.

ABOVE: *Interior, after.* The six-story atrium connecting the original building and the addition contains the elevator and a common area for residents.

RIGHT: *Arcade, after.* The arcade shields the retail space from the street and preserves the appearance of the facade.

ing for the elderly was selected, and the project began, using funds from a HUD Community Development Block Grant. The town obtained federal subsidies for the apartment units, providing a tax stabilization agreement as well as space for municipal parking. Four local banks lent money for construction costs, with an interest-rate cap on the joint loan.

The architects, John Sharratt Associates, Inc., of Boston, proposed a design that would preserve the landmark hotel while accommodating its new use and the project's financial arrangement. Its exterior details were either saved or rebuilt. No original interior details could be salvaged, because of a series of fires in the decayed building. The Second Empire architectural features were restored, and an addition was made where the movie theater had been to house some of the apartments. A six-story skylit atrium connects the two structures, and contains a common area for residents and the building's elevator. Retail space was created in the old hotel's arcade, facing Rockingham Street and the atrium. The existing structure was of brick masonry and heavy timber; the addition was constructed using similar brickwork, masonry bearing walls, and concrete floors. The new design includes a mechanical system that heats and cools the building with groundwater-source heat pumps, from a municipal "hot well" found on the site. The town of Rockingham leased access to the well, at no charge to the developer, for the duration of the project's mortgage.

These innovative and cooperative financial arrangements allowed the hotel's development, which was intended to enhance and stabilize the surrounding neighborhood. Commercial activity has been on an upswing, and future development and restoration work has been planned for the town of Rockingham. For its exemplary cooperation between the public and private sectors, and its commitment to historic preservation, the project received a 1982 Community Development Award from the U. S. Department of Housing and Urban Development.

BELOW: *Interior, after.* A rooftop terrace provides a view of downtown Bellows Falls and a sheltered area to enjoy the seasons. Throughout the restoration, features such as the scalloped slate shingles were preserved.

BELOW: *Exterior, after.* Sidewalks were replaced, and the restored arches of the facade became an arcade. The addition in the rear is new.

RIGHT: *Exterior, before.* The hotel was built in 1883 in the Victorian style, which the central business district of Bellows Falls retains today.

FAR RIGHT: *Interior, before.* A century ago, the Rockingham Hotel, with its fine restaurant, was a center of activity for local residents as well as a convenience for travelers.

THE EAGLE WAREHOUSE
BROOKLYN, NEW YORK

FROM: Warehouse storage
building
TO: Luxury apartments

The Eagle Warehouse is a group of three contiguous buildings on the Brooklyn waterfront designed by the eminent New York architect Frank Freeman. The first of the brick structures, begun in 1893, had exterior bearing walls, iron columns, and brick floor arches. A decade later, Freeman inserted new columns into the adjoining Brooklyn Eagle Printing Plant and added six floors to its existing three. (The *Brooklyn Eagle* was a prize-winning newspaper, edited for a time by Walt Whitman.) At about the same time, and on the other side, Freeman added to the Eagle with an eight-story brick-faced concrete building. The entire complex eventually served as a general warehouse, with a large part of its trade the storage of out-of-season family furnishings for Brooklyn's great and wealthy families. By 1979, the multifloor warehouse business had foundered, and a new owner engaged Rothzeid Kaiserman Thompson & Bee, P.C., to recycle the Eagle into apartments. In its final days, as a warehouse, the Eagle—serving as a Treasury Department depository for impounded marijuana—suffered the indignity of a successful heist.

Unfortunately, the Eagle, which lies just a few hundred feet upland, had almost no windows facing the river and the Manhattan skyline. After elaborate study and careful negotiations with the Landmarks Preservation Commission, Freeman's fortresslike facade was penetrated by new openings hand-cut into the yard-thick walls. Each of the three exposed facades had windows similarly installed or existing ones enlarged.

As renovated, there are eighty-five luxury apartments, simplex, duplex, and triplex, featuring elements of the bold original interior structure as well as spectacular views of the Brooklyn Bridge and the waterfront. Access is through the original Romanesque brick entrance arch and past a new nine-story atrium which contains, among other architectural artifacts, the building's "gilded cage" elevator cab, reluctantly removed from service at the insistence of building department officials. The atrium makes possible a number of floor-through units.

Of special note is the 11-foot-diameter clock, high in the north facade, whose glass face lights the first apartment to be rented.

ABOVE: *Typical, plan, after.* Hallways on three sides of the atrium connect the three buildings. Some apartments are reached by bridges through the atrium.

RIGHT: *Exterior, before.* The three-building complex served as a warehouse into the late 1970s. The nearly blank west wall, which faces Manhattan, now has many more windows.

34

RIGHT: *Exterior, after.* The north and west sides of the building. All three exposed facades had new windows installed or existing ones enlarged.

LEFT: *Atrium, after.* The air shaft between the original warehouse and the Brooklyn Eagle Printing Plant has become a nine-story atrium bridged by walkways. The "gilded cage" elevator cab is displayed in the courtyard.

BELOW: *Interior, after.* There are eighty-five luxury apartments, many with views of the East River and the Manhattan skyline.

BOTTOM: *Interior, after.* This apartment, the first to be rented, looks out through the glass front of the clock high in the north facade.

RIGHT: *Exterior, after.* Although there are still some rundown buildings nearby, the Eagle is on the riverfront of one of Brooklyn's most desirable residential neighborhoods, Brooklyn Heights.

BELOW: *Exterior, after.* The Romanesque arch of the original Eagle Warehouse remains the most striking feature from the street.

THE DANBURY MILL
D A N B U R Y , C O N N E C T I C U T

FROM: Factory
TO: Rental apartments

One headline read "Plant Wears New Hat as Condo"—a succinct description of the evolution of the Danbury Mill, a nineteenth-century hat-felting factory adapted to use as an apartment complex. Forty-one units were carved into the brick and timber structure, originally constructed in 1884. Its unknown architect built it as the factory of Peter Robinson, a Canadian who settled in Danbury in the early 1860s. The mill was used in the hatting trade, making felt from fur pelts and shaping the felt around hat molds, for nearly eighty years, and is the only one still standing.

The Danbury Mill was one of two leading fur-processing factories in the city. Located on the Still River, the mill is a large elongated building, consisting of a main block and two wings of diminishing height at its south end. The main section rises five stories and has fifteen bays and a gambrel roof. The top story and roof were constructed after a fire destroyed the original gable roof in 1895. A cornice extends around the entire building, consisting of several brick courses which are corbeled out from a brick dentil set into the wall. Flat-roofed dormers appear on either side of the gambrel roof. A tapering eight-story cylindrical smokestack featuring patterned brickwork stands behind the midsection of the plant.

Danbury was well supplied with the two basic ingredients for hatting: small fur-bearing animals and good waterpower. There were more than fifty hat factories in operation at the turn of the century, and by the 1920s and 1930s, the city was widely known as the Hat Capital of the World. However, after World War II, foreign competition increased, the hat lost its essential place in men's fashion, and the instabilities inherent in a single-

industry economy had their effect. The once familiar local slogan "Keep your neighbor working—buy a hat" no longer applied. In 1963, the building was sold to Castro Convertibles, the furniture firm, which used it as a warehouse. It later housed the Mozelle Furniture Company; chairs were manufactured on the upper levels, and showrooms occupied the ground floor.

By the 1970s, the growing service economy helped Danbury regain its former vigor. The overall decline in local industry had resulted in a surplus of large factory structures, whose conversion could satisfy the growing need for living quarters other than family homes. A study conducted by the Connecticut Department of Housing, the Connecticut Historic Commission, and the Connecticut Trust for Historic Preservation, in cooperation with the city of Danbury, identified the old mill as a prime candidate for adaptive reuse. A developer acquired the mill in November 1981 and applied to list the building in the National Register of Historic Places which would entitle the developer to a 25 percent investment tax credit for rehabilitating a historic structure, while also setting strict guidelines for the actual renovation work. The mill was listed a year later and work began that December by architects Nadler Philopena & Associates.

First, the exterior brick was cleaned with chemicals rather than sandblasting to preserve its texture and patina. All the windows on the street facade were repaired with pieces from the rear facade's windows. The windows on the rear facade were fitted with custom-crafted replicas. Over the years, a series of appendages had been added without reference to the original architectural style; the site had been totally black-

ABOVE: *Exterior, before.* The mill was built in 1884 in the Colonial style, unusual for an industrial building of the period.

BELOW: *Exterior, after.* In the rear, concrete loading docks and blacktop parking areas became private courtyards and landscaped common spaces. The windows here are replicas.

RIGHT: *Interior, after.* The once familiar local slogan, "Keep your neighbor working—buy a hat," no longer applies.

FAR RIGHT: *Interior, after.* There are forty-one rental units, from one-bedroom apartments to townhouses, each with a unique floor plan.

topped, with concrete loading docks at the rear, steel sheds along the riverfront, and parking lots on every side. Nadler Philopena selectively removed some of these late additions to reveal the original Colonial architecture—a style quite unusual for an industrial building. All but one of the sheds along the river were torn down, and the remaining one was reworked into a waterfront gazebo with lounge chairs and picnic grills. The old loading docks were converted into private courtyards and the blacktop removed to make way for landscaped plazas. The 90-foot smokestack, still in good condition, was retained as a distinctive landmark.

For the interior, one- and two-bedroom apartments, lofts, and townhouses were created. The architects retained the heavy timber posts and beams, the old (and, needless to say, exposed) brick walls, cathedral ceilings, skylights, and dormers. While boring into the basement for the elevator shaft, workers hit the wall of an underground channel that had been used to divert water into a subbasement. A water-powered turbine (a 6,000-gallon steel drum and a 6-foot cast-iron waterwheel) had been located there to generate steam and electricity for the hatting plant. This area has now been sealed off, at the request of the Connecticut Historic Commission, as an architectural "time capsule" of the area.

Ten months later, in October 1983, the Danbury Mill was fully occupied. Made economically feasible through the tax credits, the new Danbury Mill has easily taken shape within the last major remnant of the Danbury hatting industry of the late nineteenth and early twentieth centuries.

BULFINCH SQUARE
EAST CAMBRIDGE , MASSACHUSETTS

FROM: County courthouse
TO: Offices, restaurant,
gallery, theater

In 1973, the Middlesex County Courthouse buildings, whose rich architectural heritage includes the initial design in 1814 by Charles Bulfinch (1763–1844), the first American-born architect, were scheduled to be razed to make way for a parking lot.

The courthouse site in East Cambridge has been controversial for almost two centuries. East Cambridge today joins seamlessly with the rest of Cambridge and neighboring Boston, but was in the early 1800s an isolated marshland. In 1809 Andrew Craigie constructed a bridge linking East Cambridge to Boston and formed a group of investors, the Lechmere Point Corporation, in an effort to further general development of the area. They encountered opposition and debate by donating the land and funding for the building, and persuaded the reluctant county commissioners to move the courthouse to East Cambridge. One hundred and sixty years later, following the construction of a new courthouse nearby, Graham Gund provided the impetus to persuade various government officials and agencies to cancel the planned demolition of the buildings and support its adaptive reuse as a multicultural arts center and office space.

Since its original construction, the Middlesex County Courthouse has been in an almost perpetual state of change. There remains only one sketch of the original courthouse. The restored center section of the five interconnected buildings, occupying a city block, was patterned after this sketch and is reminiscent of the Bulfinch original. In 1848, Ammi B. Young, the architect of Boston's Custom House, expanded the courthouse by adding two-story wings to the original

RIGHT: *Interior, after.* Today, those who visit Bulfinch Square hear musical recitals rather than court testimony.

40

BELOW: *Exterior, after.* Renovation of the former Middlesex County Courthouse buildings has given East Cambridge a focus for broader neighborhood improvement.

RIGHT: *Interior, during renovation.* The seal by John Garvey was one of the many plaster embellishments that was carefully restored.

FAR RIGHT: *Interior, after.* A century and a half of public use had left the interior in disrepair, and restoration required research and good craftsmanship as well as concern for the integrity of the historic structure.

ABOVE: *Interior, after.* This former courtroom will become an architect's studio; other spaces in the building will be used for a theater and offices.

building and incorporating a Greek Revival portico in the main facade. Interior embellishments included a large plaster seal in one courtroom done by John Garvey of New York, who also worked with Young on the Custom House. In 1877, space demands required construction of another building, and in 1899, construction of the Probate and Insolvent Courts building necessitated moving the 1877 structure back 37 feet. In 1901, the more recent buildings were connected, and in 1924, the linkage was expanded. Then in 1970 a new Middlesex County Courthouse was built, leaving the old courthouses vacant.

Graham Gund, architect of the restored Bulfinch Square, has said that he viewed the courthouses as a unique opportunity to save buildings that few others saw as worthwhile. This project is a representative one for his firm, which has undertaken several high-risk ventures in marginal neighborhoods.

The first step toward renovation was to place the courthouse on the National Register of Historic Places. The 1924 addition, which obscured a nineteenth-century facade, was demolished, and, using an 1848 lithograph, the architect reconstructed the original portico and restored the landscaping. The resulting outdoor space ties into the Lechmere Canal Park System. Further exterior work included the cleaning and repair of original brickwork, cast-iron trim, wrought-iron fencing, slate roofs, and copper roof cresting. The gold dome atop the Bulfinch building was regilded, the landmark clock tower was restored and its faces repainted, and the 1,000-pound bell was electrified.

The interior reconstruction was equally challenging, because much of the decoration was in disrepair or had been removed. Careful research, attention to detail, and fine craftsmanship returned the major courtrooms to their original elegance, and new construction was completed with care for the integrity of the historic structure. Existing paneled doors and frames, plaster friezes and moldings, marble floors, and cast-iron staircases were repaired. The final product is a unique combination of restored courtrooms and renovated space adapted for use as a theater, offices, and a restaurant. Gund himself plans to relocate his offices to the Bulfinch building, using two of the restored courtrooms as architectural studios.

In 1814, Bulfinch was paid $100 for his plans. In 1984, the cost of restoration was approximately $10 million.

TOP: *Exterior, after.* The portico is a reconstruction of an 1848 addition by Ammi B. Young. The renovation architect, Graham Gund, based his restoration of the courthouse exterior on an 1848 lithograph.

ABOVE: *Interior, after.* Existing woodwork, cast-iron staircases, friezes, and other fine features were repaired and restored.

RIGHT: *Exterior, after.* At one point Charles Bulfinch's 1814 courthouse was to be razed. It still stands, and the scales of justice still ornament the clock tower.

LIBRARY HALL
EASTON, PENNSYLVANIA

FROM: Library, dental office, union hall
TO: Architectural offices

TOP: *Exterior, before.* The two-story structure contained four major reading rooms. Of note were the two Palladian windows and entrance-door transom.

ABOVE: *Interior, after.* George Taylor, signer of the Declaration of Independence, lived in Easton—one of the first cities where the document was read.

Lechauwitank, meaning "the place at the forks," is the name the Delaware Indians gave to the site where Easton, Pennsylvania, now stands. The strategic location, on a bluff overlooking the Delaware River, also appealed to Thomas Penn (son of William Penn), who founded the town there in 1752. During the American Revolution, Easton was an important economic center and a vital military depot. George Taylor, a signer of the Declaration of Independence, lived there—in fact, Easton was one of the first cities where that document was read publicly.

With such geographic significance, and historic and commercial prominence, it is not surprising that the residents of Easton had a flourishing cultural life. In 1811, the Library Company, a private dues-paying group modeled after the Library Company in Philadelphia, was founded under the leadership of Samuel Sitgreaves, whose personal collection formed the nucleus of the new library. At first the group met in each other's homes, but in April 1814 they purchased a small building near the corner of Fermor (now 2nd) Street and Church Alley. A new Federal-style building was built over, and around, the existing small structure. The basement of that older house still exists under the central part of the present building, and the old brick walls were incorporated into the new interior walls. Although the original architect is unknown, he clearly modeled his

design after Library Hall and Carpenters' Hall in Philadelphia. The structure had a particularly handsome front elevation, with Palladian windows and a matching entrance door transom, and contained four major reading rooms on two stories.

Since this was a private library, it was necessary to have an appointment from the library committee to use the collection. Eventually the original members of the Library Company died, and there were few new members to take their place. In 1864, the library was taken over by the Easton School Board, who ran it as a public facility. When a new library building was constructed nearly forty years later, Library Hall became the administrative offices of the school district and a meeting place for the school board. During the school board's tenure at Library Hall, decorative wooden cornice brackets were installed on the exterior, and the interior staircase was "modernized" in the Victorian style, with a new handrail and balusters. It was common practice during that time to change earlier, simple staircases into newer, more fashionable ones, since the advent of mechanization had made it both cheap and easy to turn fancier balusters. With one small change, a new stair hall could give a building an "up-to-date" look.

In 1964, a dentist, Dr. Henry Ungerleiter, bought the building from the school and converted it into a dental office, partitioning off one of the reading rooms and replacing the front double doors

RIGHT: *Exterior, during renovation.* The unknown architect seemingly based his design on Philadelphia's Library Hall and Carpenters' Hall.

with a single one. He sold the building in 1972 to an electrical workers' union, which added new paneling and dropped ceilings. Archive, a restoration design consulting firm, bought Library Hall in 1984 and have begun a five-year effort to restore the building to its original state, for use as its own offices.

The owner-architect, Jeffrey Gilbert, and his partner, Oliver Andes, have undertaken to restore Library Hall to an exact replica of its original Federal-style appearance. Remarkably, few major architectural changes had been made. Authentic historical details include replacement of newer light fixtures with more appropriate wooden chandeliers in the reception room, and duplication of window aprons and baseboards that had been torn out when the paneling was installed. All the original woodwork has been stripped of accumulated layers of paint and is now being repainted in the Federal style of gray with black pinstripes. A boarded-up oculus window on the facade is being reglazed, and more appropriate double doors will replace the existing single front door.

Now a popular stop on the tour of Easton's Old City historic district, known for its many fine examples of Victorian architecture, Library Hall was awarded a design commendation by Historic Easton, a preservation group formed to encourage individuals, businesses, and investors to help bring this city's past back to life.

THE RUSSELL HOUSE
MIDDLETOWN, CONNECTICUT

FROM: Residence, fraternity
house
TO: Wesleyan University
offices

TOP AND ABOVE: *Exterior, before and after.* Although the Greek Revival entrance was basically intact, it bore the marks of half a century of fraternity use.

The Russell House, an elegant example of Greek Revival-style architecture was used, and nearly ruined, by Wesleyan University's "Greeks." It evolved from a private residence to a fraternity house, until the university rescued it and converted it into its development office.

The Russell House was built in 1841–1842 for Edward Augustus Russell, member of a distinguished Middletown family that had resided there since the seventeenth century. In 1825, Edward joined his older brother, Samuel, in China, working as a trader for Russell & Company, which Samuel founded. Edward returned to Middletown in 1838. He served as mayor from 1858 to 1861, and later as a state representative. His business interests included the directorship of several railroads and the presidency of the Charles River Railroad in Massachusetts. In spite of this impressive career, Edward was never as financially successful as his brother Samuel, who often came to his brother's aid, and even provided the money to build Edward's home.

In 1874 at age seventy-seven, Edward died and passed the house on to his widow and two maiden daughters (his two sons had died some time before). His eldest daughter, Mary, married Edward deZeng; their son, Richard deZeng, occupied the house until he died in 1932. Two years later the property was purchased by Wesleyan University and sold to the Alpha Sigma Delta Alumni Association.

In its incarnation as a fraternity house, the Russell House underwent some physical changes (and atmospheric ones, to be sure). Its cornice was lowered so that larger windows could be installed on the third floor, and the attic was converted into rooms. A three-story fire escape was added at the rear of the building, extending over the back porch, which was partially enclosed at that time. The rooms on the main floor, containing several marble fireplaces, were not greatly altered, except for the partitioning of one into several smaller rooms, one of which extended a few feet beyond the original line of the building. The second and third floors were extensively remodeled into nine bedrooms.

By 1983, the Russell House bore the marks of fraternity-house living: the doorway columns were decaying, the main staircase was missing many of its banister poles, the interior paint and wallpaper were peeling, and the whole exterior was covered with graying, chipping paint.

The building was purchased by the university from Kappa Nu Kappa Fraternity in 1983 and then sold to a limited partnership to be restored to its original elegance. Jeter, Cook & Jepson, P.C., were retained, and under the provisions of the Economic Recovery Tax Act of 1981, the building was restored and leased back to the university for use.

The facade of the Russell House is a simple rectangle, displaying a spare sense of geometry.

RIGHT: *Exterior, before.* Completed in 1842, the Russell House was a private home until it became a fraternity house in the 1930s.

BELOW: *Exterior, after.* Removal of the third-floor windows installed by the fraternity and restoration of the screened pediment brought elegance back to the facade.

Its pediment is pierced with openwork screens with organic motifs, which are repeated in the design of the first-floor window grilles. An oval window also graces the lower floor. The entrance is surrounded by two Tuscan-style pilasters and two freestanding Ionic columns, surmounted by a classical cornice with egg-and-dart molding similar to the main cornice that encircles the building. The wood-frame structure has flush wood siding with lath plastering. It rests on a brownstone foundation.

During restoration, the cornice was raised to its original height, the screens were replaced in the pediment, and exterior and interior features were repaired and repainted. The goal was to restore as many of the original architectural features as possible—features that were symbolic of changing cultural and aesthetic tastes of the period, from grand Greek temple styles to simpler Greek domestic styles.

The building now serves as the University Relations office. Its original floor plan remains. The main foyer has been repainted so that the delicate Greek Revival garlands along the molding are visible. The freestanding main staircase has been repaired and polished. Offices fit comfortably into the well-lit rooms. The house forms part of a row of four High Street homes owned by Wesleyan that are all on the National Register of Historic Places.

THE FORMER POLICE HEADQUARTERS

NEW YORK, NEW YORK

FROM: Police Headquarters
TO: Residential lofts, community cultural center, restaurant, and other commercial space

TOP: *Interior, before.* Designers L. DePolo/ Dunbar Inc. and architects Ehrenkrantz Group P.C. hope to restore the building to its original Edwardian Baroque magnificence.

ABOVE: *Interior, before.* The police department moved out in 1973, but renovation did not begin until 1985.

The Police Headquarters, a grandiose Edwardian Baroque structure, on a wedge-shaped site in downtown New York City, is a testimonial to the history of one of the nation's largest and most sophisticated police forces. In 1798, in an effort to complement the traditional "Night Watch," the first police department was established at City Hall. Within eight years New York City's population had increased fifty-six times, which contributed to an increased crime rate. In 1862, the police department moved from City Hall to a building at 300 Mulberry Street, where politicians such as Chester A. Arthur and Ulysses S. Grant would come to learn the results of the city's elections. It is believed that this is where "third-degree" questioning originated. By 1900, the police department had quadrupled in an attempt to control the rapidly increasing crime rate. In 1901, all responsibility for administering the city's law enforcement organization was given to a single police commissioner.

In 1903, the architectural firm Hoppin and Koen produced drawings for the new headquarters to be built where the Old Market Place, a Greek Revival building designed in 1838 by Thomas Thomas, the founder of the American Institute of Architects, had stood since 1817. Contemporary taste in municipal architecture favored Beaux-Arts classicism, the English "Wren-naissance";

English municipal buildings such as Old Bailey (1900-1907), Scotland Yard's headquarters, and Edward Mountford's Central Criminal Courts all influenced the design for the new headquarters.

The main facade of the five-story granite-and-limestone building features a central pedimented pavilion topped by a dome and balanced by two end pavilions. A central three-part rusticated arcade adorned with decorative iron grilles by Harris H. Uris Iron Works supports monumental Corinthian columns, which in turn sustain the central portico. A bas-relief of New York City's seal fills the pediment, and on top of the gable sits an allegorical figure of Manhattan. Baroque touches such as the two domed towers that flank the main portico, enhanced by caryatids and clocks set in *oeils-de-boeuf* (circular windows), complement the classical composition. The end pavilions are surmounted by low domes gilded and paneled in the Austrian Rococo manner.

Upon its completion in 1909, the Police Headquarters was hailed as the most advanced facility in the country. The police commissioner could enter the building in a motor car; a private elevator took him to his office. (This was the office Theodore Roosevelt might have occupied had he not gone on to higher echelons of public service. He served as police commissioner from 1885 to 1887.) The building also featured an 80- by 120-

RIGHT: *Exterior, before.* The design was influenced by English municipal buildings and is reminiscent of Old Bailey, completed in 1907.

BELOW: *Interior, after, renderings.* The former main entrance to the Police Headquarters will become the residential entrance, with a concierge desk. The residential units will have a wide range of sizes and layouts.

foot Drill Room with an elevated running track. In the basement there was a 130-foot pistol range. The Trial Room is almost as large as the ones used by the Supreme Court.

When the police department moved to One Police Plaza in 1973, the building remained vacant for four years. In 1977, the city leased the building to the Little Italy Restoration Association for $1 a year, for use as the Little Italy International Cultural Center. LIRA failed to maintain or improve the structure, and the lease was terminated in March 1980. The General Services Administration sent out requests for proposals to 640 developers. A proposal by TransNation, a Canada-based company, to convert the building into a 125-room "Grand Hotel de Ville" was accepted, but when the Canadian government froze the company's assets these plans fell through. Then, in November 1983, the Jeffersonian Corporation proposed to convert the building into sixty residential apartments, a community cultural center, and commercial spaces. The designers, L. DePolo/Dunbar, Inc., and the architects, Ehrenkrantz Group, P.C., have as their first priority the restoration of the building to its original magnificence, retaining as much of the original detailing as possible while providing a wide range of apartment sizes and configurations to suit varied market requirements. Construction began in the spring of 1986.

THE WATSON STUDIO
NEW YORK, NEW YORK

FROM: Meat-processing plant
TO: Photographer's studio
and residence

Greenwich Village is one of the oldest sections of Manhattan; it contains the greatest concentration of early New York residential architecture to be found anywhere within the city's five boroughs. No single block or individual landmark can adequately express the neighborhood's character or spirit; therefore, in 1969, the Landmarks Preservation Commission of the city of New York designated all of Greenwich Village a historic district. In 1948, when a meat-processing plant opened its doors on the western edge of Greenwich Village, it must have seemed unlikely to any of its workers—or to the residents of what was then a working-class neighborhood— that it would one day be a part of a historic district—or be the studio and residence of a New York photographer.

Randolph Croxton, the architect, and his client, Albert Watson, a fashion photographer, actually went "shopping" for the building. Watson required a large space with good light; Croxton preferred a deteriorated building in a landmark district. The building they eventually selected was fairly nondescript, its original architect unknown and its plans long lost, but Croxton's adaptive redesign for the building retained its essentially industrial character and elegance.

Before the renovation began, many of the windows on the Jane Street side of the building had been blocked; Croxton opened them up with "interpretive" replacement windows, double-glazed and steel-framed, incorporating elements of in-

dustrial function with residential beauty and utility. Concrete patches on the floor, once used to support heavy machinery, were removed and the floor was leveled. Many of the advertising signs were retained, however, some of them illustrating the plant's slaughter booth and blood-draining vats. The architect also broke through the ground floor to the basement to provide his client with higher ceilings and better lighting. The portion of the building now used as the studio was once a garage and has direct access to the street; now, automobiles and other large objects used in photographic sessions can be brought into a studio measuring 32 by 76 feet, with 18-foot ceilings.

The exterior of the building remains consistent with residential dwellings on the same block; wrought-iron fences and planters have been introduced. Additional new square footage accommodates the photographer's residence. The penthouse, a 10-foot extension including a deck, an atrium, and skylights, serves as the living space. To maintain the original street line, the three-story cornice has been matched and the penthouse extension inset and covered in stucco to be less imposing. The effect is the addition of height and bulk without distortion of the building's proportions.

The Watson Studio is a successful adaptation of an industrial building that respects its original function, while enhancing what is now an increasingly residential historic neighborhood.

ABOVE: *Exterior, before.* Windows were irregularly shaped and sized, and many had been blocked up.

BELOW: *Exterior, during renovation.* Above the ground floor, the arched windows, pierced balustrades, and copper-roofed dormers remain as architects Kimball & Thompson designed them in the 1890s.

RIGHT: *Exterior, before.* The original entrance was recreated in the center of the Madison Avenue facade, modeled after this long-lost photograph.

FAR RIGHT: *Exterior, before.* The mansion was built for Gertrude Rhinelander Waldo, who never lived in it; it was not occupied until 1920, twenty-two years after its completion.

cealed behind the cabinetry and fixtures. The first floor and the Grand Salon on the second floor house menswear. The Ballroom and the rest of the third floor are allocated to women's clothing. The fourth floor is devoted to accessories and home furnishings.

The exterior renovation was an elaborate undertaking. In the years immediately before the project began, the main floor was shared by several retail operations, each of which had a separate entrance and storefront. The designers, in an attempt to recall the original building, have removed the commercial entrances and replaced them with windows set into the stone of the building. The original entrance has been re-created in the center of the Madison Avenue facade—it is carved five feet into the stone wall and modeled after a photograph that was discovered. There is evidence that parts of the building were truncated; the areas above the northern and southern balustrades project over the areas beneath them. It is speculated this was done either because the mansion extended past the building line or because Madison Avenue was widened after the mansion was completed.

The Waldo Rhinelander Mansion promises to be a wonderful place to work and shop, enhanced by its colorful history and superb architecture.

THE PALLADIUM
NEW YORK, NEW YORK

FROM: Theater and concert hall
TO: Discotheque/nightclub

ABOVE: *Interior, after.* A phone booth—one of the intentions of the discotheque is to offer art to the public in unusual forms.

RIGHT: *Interior, after.* The dance floor is lit not by strobes but by "varilights," which can produce sixty variations of color in a quarter of a second.

In May 1985, an unconventional club called the Palladium opened in New York City. Those who can get past the door encounter theatrical sets by Keith Haring, complimentary drink tickets by Andy Warhol, recreation rooms by Kenny Scharf, and much more. This new discotheque intends to offer the public an art experience in a way not available in traditional galleries or museums; it even has its own art director, Henry Geldzahler, former curator of twentieth-century art at New York's Metropolitan Museum of Art. The club attempts to synthesize art, architecture, design, music, and fashion. In fact, the Palladium was masterminded as a fusion of fine art and pop art, as a junction (because of its 14th Street location) of downtown creativity and uptown sophistication.

The Palladium began as the Academy of Music opera house. The Academy of Music was first built across the street, in 1854, when 14th Street was part of Peter Stuyvesant's sizable farm. In 1866 a fire leveled the building, and a new, larger theater was erected on the site. This building was demolished and rebuilt on the present site in 1926. From 1926 to 1983, when it was purchased by a group of business executives, the Academy of Music served as opera house, ballroom, burlesque theater, and rock concert hall. While its most recent transformation is visually more spectacular, entertainment is certainly not new to the Palladium—it was always a palatial pleasure center.

Japanese architect Arata Isozaki, designed the Palladium. To preserve the building's historical integrity, he proceeded to erect a structure within a structure. The dilapidated exterior, complete with

BELOW: *Interior, after.* Isozaki's bold additions and the preserved-yet-worn interior that encloses them, though hardly in conventional harmony, seem to strengthen each other.

RIGHT: *Exterior, after.* The Palladium occupies the old Academy of Music building on East 14th Street, formerly the northern boundary of Manhattan's "bohemian" neighborhoods.

FAR RIGHT: *Interior, after.* This eerie corridor was designed by Kenny Scharf.

shabby marquee, was retained as the shell for a dramatically high-tech, visually dazzling interior. The 120-foot-long lobby was designed to create an underwater atmosphere, with an undulating wall, turquoise and purple carpeting, and a low ceiling to establish the feeling of compression. The most striking feature of the lobby is the sleek double staircase, built of glass blocks lit from underneath with 2,400 lights. The idea for the illuminated glass blocks was inspired by the sidewalks of SoHo, where in the nineteenth century similar blocks provided light to cellars extending beyond the building lines.

The club's next story houses the dance floor. No blinking strobe lights for the Palladium's dancers. The floor is lit by the world's first permanent installation of "varilights"; each light can produce sixty variations of color within a quarter second. Two four-ton video banks, each with twenty-five monitors encased in a frame shaped like a Rolls-Royce grille, swivel over the dance floor, creating moving walls of video images.

In spite of all this sleek, futuristic architecture and the award-winning lighting design by Paul Marantz, the interior is not entirely new. Huge, ornate cartouches still adorn some walls. Old theater seats ascend to the top of the balcony; sitting atop all the movement and excitement, one still feels like a spectator in a theater, watching a spectacular, if idiosyncratic, show. The Mike Todd Room, named after the famous theater and movie producer and located just beyond the balcony, is another remnant of the old theater. The room is meant to resemble a speakeasy, with tables covered in white lace, elaborate candelabras, gilt-edged mirrors, a mahogany bar, and leather banquettes. The rusting pipes and steel girders were deliberately left exposed and in their rusted condition. The room's crumbling walls remain unrepaired, but they now boast two new Jean-Michel Basquiat murals. For all its decayed atmosphere, the room achieves a sense of eerie elegance; it might have made an excellent setting for Miss Havisham in *Great Expectations*. The Mike Todd Room epitomizes the two extremes juxtaposed in the club. Here art and elegance are contrasted with deterioration and decay in order to symbolize the essence of the new club—as well as something of New York's ever-changing style and spirit. The club's premise is the fusion of disparate elements, including the merging of selective landmark restoration and futuristic architecture.

ABOVE: *Interior, after.* The old opera house's ornate plasterwork is overlaid here with a mural by Francesco Clemente.

RIGHT: *Interior, after.* The double staircase in the lobby is lighted from below through glass blocks—a reversal of the nineteenth-century practice of illuminating subgrade cellar extensions by glass blocks set in the sidewalk.

BELOW: *Interior, after.* The discotheque has its own art director, Henry Geldzahler, formerly a curator at New York's Metropolitan Museum of Art.

RIGHT: *Interior, after.* In the Mike Todd Room the crumbling walls were not repaired but designed to exaggerate the combined decay and elegance of the former opera house.

FAR RIGHT: *Interior, after.* The lighting, which in a discotheque is an important part of the design, was created by Paul Marantz.

ABOVE: *Interior, after.* Architect Arata Isozaki built a new and radical structure within the original ornate and decaying structure.

RIGHT: *Interior, after.* The suspended banks of video monitors weigh four tons each.

THE JAYNE HOUSE
PHILADELPHIA, PENNSYLVANIA

FROM: Residence, offices
TO: Law offices

The Jayne House was built in 1895 for Dr. Horace Jayne, a Philadelphia physician with an auspicious family background. His great-uncle was William Henry Furness, a Unitarian minister, abolitionist, champion of the arts, and noted public speaker. William Henry Furness had three sons, all of whom had established reputations in their chosen professions: William Henry Furness, Jr., was a well-known portrait painter, Horace Howard Furness (Dr. Jayne's father-in-law) was a lawyer and a published Shakespearean scholar, and Frank Furness was a distinguished High Victorian architect; he designed the Jayne House for his niece's husband, among many other buildings, during his 45-year-long career.

Frank Furness (1839–1912) was a dominant force in Philadelphia architecture. After apprenticing in William Morris Hunt's atelier, he opened his own office in 1865 and became known nationally for the singularity of his work, its Victorian-influenced creativity, power, and eclecticism. Among his major works are the Pennsylvania Academy of Fine Arts (1871–1876), the Furness Library at the University of Pennsylvania (1888–1891), the Pennsylvania Railroad Station at Broad Street (1892–1893), as well as the B&O and Reading railroad stations, and numerous homes and bank buildings in Philadelphia. In the midst of these major commissions, Frank Furness built the Jayne House, a Victorian building of red brick and stone which housed Dr. Jayne's family, as well as his practice, for thirty-three years.

The house was purchased in 1928 by Jacob Lit, a merchant whose Lit Brothers Department Store competed with the better-known department stores such as Wanamaker's, Gimbels, and Strawbridge's in the late nineteenth and early twentieth centuries. During the Lit family's residency, modifications were made on the interior, but the Furness exterior was left intact. Steam radiators for the heating system were installed and covered with attractively designed iron "borzoi"—Russian wolfhound—convector covers. In the main dining room, the Victorian-style interior was removed and replaced with cherry paneling in a Colonial Revival style. An elevator was added in the southeast corner of the building; it destroyed three major rooms, closed off windows, and cut into three fireplace mantels.

On the second floor, a stairway was constructed from Mrs. Lit's bedroom to the nursery above. This addition, designed as a safety precaution, was prompted by the Lindbergh kidnapping. The only way to reach the child upstairs was through the mother's bedroom.

Further structural changes followed when, in 1952, the building was sold to a center city synagogue. Many of its main rooms, such as the drawing room, reception room, and library, were revised to adapt them for religious purposes. More alterations were made in the 1960s when the building was sold to the Heart Association of Southeastern Pennsylvania. To adapt the house for "modern" office use, they added fluorescent lighting and movable partitions to create a series of office cubicles. The main hall's fireplace mirror and mantel were stripped and covered over, and two doorways opposite it were closed off. Upstairs, rooms were divided and ceilings lowered, and brass wall sconces and other fixtures were painted over.

BELOW: *Exterior, after.* Despite nearly half a century of interior modifications, the facade remained as Furness designed it.

RIGHT: *Exterior, during construction in 1895.* The eminent High Victorian architect Frank Furness designed the house for Dr. Horace Jayne, his nephew.

FAR RIGHT: *Interior, during renovation.* The architect was Hyman Myers, a restoration specialist. The project took nine months and cost about $500,000.

ABOVE: *Interior, before.* During its tenure the Heart Association of Southeastern Pennsylvania added fluorescent lighting and partitions to create office cubicles.

When the current developer/owners bought the property in 1982, the building was in great need of repair. The windows were drafty, the roof needed replacing, the plumbing and heating systems were inefficient and leaky, the interior plasterwork was cracked, and other interior finishes had been stripped away. Hyman Myers, restoration architect, set out to adapt the space into offices for a small law firm and to restore the light, open-air quality of this grand Victorian building. A suite of offices was created for each of the four law partners, as well as a central reception area, an atriumlike hall topped by an ornamental glass skylight, to unify the suites, and common areas for office functions and conference rooms. The formerly unfinished basement areas now house the law library, mail room, staff lounge and kitchen, and storage and mechanical spaces. Fireplaces and their mantels were restored, and the intrusive south elevator was removed. A balcony overlooks the reception hall, from which one can see the second-floor corridor, suspended by iron bars from the floor above. What was formerly Mrs. Lit's bedroom became the central room

in a partner suite, containing the Lindbergh stairway. Now closed off at the ceiling, but kept intact, "the stair to nowhere" adds an interesting, if curious, design element to the room.

In Mr. Lit's bedroom, now the central room of a partner suite, a double-door entrance was installed using doors and even door trim found in the basement. The suite above Mrs. Lit's old bedroom has been restored to its original Furness form, without the stair and railing from below. The room gains its character from the many folds in its ceiling, caused by the steeply sloped roof intersected by dormers. Outside this room is a new roof deck which is not visible from the street and therefore preserves the building's original facade.

Throughout the building, as much of the original detailing as possible was re-created: wood paneling, leaded casement windows, and ornamental wood and plaster designs to revive its Victorian atmosphere. The entire project was completed in nine months and cost approximately $500,000—a fee hardly comparable to that paid by Dr. Jayne to his uncle Frank Furness in 1895.

TOP: *Interior, after.* This partner suite was formerly a bedroom; the stairway, now closed off at the ceiling, was the only entrance to a child's bedroom—an addition prompted by the Lindbergh kidnapping.

ABOVE: *Interior, after.* A suite was created for each of the four partners of the law firm that owns the building.

RIGHT: *Interior, after.* In the skylit reception area, as elsewhere, the architect restored or re-created as much as possible of the Victorian woodwork.

THE OLD POST OFFICE
WASHINGTON, D.C.

FROM: Postal Service head-quarters, government offices
TO: Offices and arcade

Finally, after more than a decade of planning, Washington's abandoned Old Post Office is filled with people working, playing, or doing a little of both. Located on Pennsylvania Avenue and listed on the National Register of Historic Places, the building currently houses the offices of the National Endowments for the Arts and Humanities, the Advisory Council on Historic Preservation, and an assortment of restaurants and shops in its newly constructed atrium.

The Old Post Office building was originally completed in 1899 and served as the headquarters for the United States Postal Service until 1934. In two governmental attempts to complete the Federal Triangle (including the Mall's National Archives and Justice Department) in the Classical Revival style, early promoters of the Triangle felt the Romanesque post office, built by Willoughby J. Edbrooke, would have to go. His design was considered a "cross between a cathedral and a cotton mill," and the building was known as the Old Tooth for its soaring clock tower. The Depression and World War II postponed its destruction. For the next forty-three years, it was occupied by various government agencies, including the FBI's wiretapping unit. When in 1969 the General Services Administration again proposed completing the Triangle, with the construction of an extension to the existing Internal Revenue Service building, it requested the Advisory Council's comments. The GSA plan was to save only the Old Post Office's fourteen-story clock tower, a local landmark and the tallest edifice in downtown Washington except for the Washington Monument, and tear down the rest. The council considered the project at its meeting in February 1970, but deferred a decision until further information was available. No conclusions were drawn until the council's May 1971 meeting, when it was recommended that the Old Post Office be preserved in its entirety and that the GSA solicit plans for its preservation. Not until the summer of 1977 did GSA select a design team to develop renovation plans, with construction of the $30 million renovation to begin in 1978.

The renovation was the flagship project of the Cooperative Use Act of 1976, which permits mixed uses in federal buildings. Washington architects John Wiebenson and Arthur Cotton Moore shared their ideas on the scope of possibilities for the Old Post Office. They believed the building could become both a symbol and generator of diversity in a place where the city needed it most.

Edbrooke's original design, executed in gray Maine granite, proved difficult to work with. Described as a rectangular doughnut, the building had a vast skylit courtyard surrounded by office corridors. Its ground floor, formerly used as a mail-sorting center, was covered with a glazed truss, so that only the office workers had a view of the soaring courtyard space, whose glass roof had been painted black. Arthur Cotton Moore, whose firm eventually won the architectural competition to restore the building, felt Edbrooke's design had never really worked as well as it could have. Moore's solution was to open the courtyard space by breaking through to the basement level with a sweeping staircase and installing an arcade.

The three-level Pavilion shopping area steps back in a sequence of curves ("like tiers in an

ABOVE: *Exterior, before.* About 1909. The tower is the tallest structure in downtown Washington except for the Washington Monument.

RIGHT: *Exterior, before.* A parade passes the Old Post Office in 1919, after the Great War ended.

BELOW: *Exterior, after.* Architect Willoughby J. Edbrooke's Romanesque Post Office, three times slated for demolition, endures, and now houses the NEA, the NEH, and the Advisory Council on Historic Preservation.

TOP: *Atrium, after.* Looking down from the office levels, the tiered design of the Pavilion is apparent. It contains twenty-one restaurants and twenty-nine specialty shops.

ABOVE: *Atrium, after.* Architect Arthur Cotton Moore removed glazing from the trusses and glazed the formerly opaque roof high above the courtyard.

RIGHT: *Atrium, after.* At the far end of the courtyard is the granite footing of the clock tower, and the tower itself is visible through the roof. Offices rise above the three-level Pavilion.

ABOVE: *Exterior, after.* The Pavilion contains 60,000 square feet of retail space. The Old Post Office was the first public federal building ever restored for mixed private and government use.

LEFT: *Exterior, after.* The broad plaza along Pennsylvania Avenue is used for café seating. The clock tower contains replicas of the bells in Westminster Abbey, a bicentennial gift from Great Britain.

opera house") from the central clock tower. The tower's base, excavated to reveal its granite footings, forms the background for this semicircular arena. The truss was opened and refurbished, and the glass above the ten-story courtyard replaced, lighting the whole interior. The retail space (60,000 square feet) of the Pavilion, designed by the Cambridge, Massachusetts, firm of Benjamin Thompson & Associates, contains twenty-nine specialty shops and twenty-one restaurants, including five full-service establishments. It was finished in marble and tile, with brass fittings, red oak woodwork, and frosted glass. A glass-encased elevator within the atrium takes visitors up to the tower's viewing platform, an addition to Washington's numerous tourist attractions. The tower also contains a set of bells, a bicentennial gift from the Ditchley Foundation of Great Britain and replicas of those in Westminster Abbey.

Architect Moore, whose initial volunteer proposal was to turn the building into a hotel, conceived of the center as active both day and night, and to this end took advantage of its location and architectural character. The back of the building, facing 12th Street, was transformed from an ordinary loading dock into an interesting entrance halfway between Pennsylvania Avenue and the Mall. There is another entrance at its northeast corner, near Pennsylvania Avenue. Moore's strategic plan allows the building to act as a bridge between the Mall and the city, the first step toward this junction since the federal government began clearing the land for the Triangle's neoclassical office buildings in the late 1930s.

The new Old Post Office has been compared to Baltimore's Harborplace and Boston's Faneuil Hall. Given certain statistics—twenty million tourists on the Mall, 115,000 office workers within four blocks of the building—a market existed for the kind of complex created in the Old Post Office. And the Pavilion has been busy since its opening in 1983. Officially named the Nancy Hanks Center, in honor of the late chairperson of the National Endowment for the Arts and strong supporter of the District of Columbia preservation group, named "Don't Tear It Down," which lobbied long to see the building reused, the Old Post Office is a key element in the continuing revitalization along Pennsylvania Avenue between the Capitol and the White House. As the first public building ever restored for mixed use, combining federal office space, shops, eateries, and the performing arts, the Old Post Office should impress the bureaucracy that three times slated it for demolition with its tenacity and vibrancy.

RIGHT: *Exterior, after.* The Pennsylvania Avenue facade.

BELOW: *Exterior, after.* Completed in 1899, the Old Post Office was headquarters for the U.S. Postal Service until 1934 and then was used by various government agencies.

THE SEARS HEADQUARTERS BUILDING
WASHINGTON, D.C.

FROM: Three distinct buildings; studios, commercial
TO: Integrated structure; corporate headquarters

The Executive Divisional Headquarters for Sears, Roebuck & Co. —one of the largest department store chains in the country— is now located in what used to be three distinct nineteenth-century landmark buildings, situated on Pennsylvania Avenue, Pierre L'Enfant's symbolic link between the executive and legislative branches of the federal government. The new headquarters, located on a trapezoidal area divided as four lots, comprises the Apex Building and the Italianate Mathew Brady and Gilman structures.

The Apex Building, built in 1860 and originally the St. Mark's Hotel, is one of the earliest examples of fire-resistant construction in Washington, with ashlar walls and shallow plastered brick vaults spanning rolled-iron beams on the first floor. The original architects are not known, but Alfred B. Mullet, supervising architect of the Treasury, made major renovations in 1888 for its use as the Central National Bank. He added the twin six-story towers and a new facade for the west elevation, as well as ground floors for the north and south elevations. Mullet's work for the Treasury Department includes many significant federal buildings throughout the country, such as the State, War and Navy Building, adjacent to the White House, now known as the Executive Office Building. In later years, the Apex Building housed a liquor store.

Neighboring the Apex Building are two commercial Italianate buildings, one of which was Gilman's drugstore, built in 1854. When Gilman's closed in 1965, it had been the oldest drugstore in continuous operation (1843-1965) in the United States. The other structure, built about 1840, was once the studio of the famous Civil War

RIGHT: *Exterior, after.* The Apex Building was built in 1860; the twin-towered west facade was added in 1888 when the former hotel became the Central National Bank.

RIGHT: *Exterior, after.* The porticoed central structure is new; it connects the buildings that now are a Sears, Roebuck headquarters and houses elevators and other necessary core elements.

ABOVE: *Interior, after.* The cast-iron staircase was relocated; it originally ascended to the second floor and now descends to basement conference rooms.

photographer Mathew Brady, and was one of the first photographic studios in Washington. From 1858 to 1881 it served as the home of the National Photographic Gallery.

In 1982 an innovative restoration project began, under the jurisdiction of the Pennsylvania Avenue Development Corporation, to convert the buildings for use as the Sears World Headquarters. An infill building was erected, connecting the existing buildings, in the narrow lot separating the Apex Building from the Gilman and Brady structures. It provided space for needed core elements (restrooms, elevators, an additional fire stair). The differing floor heights of the connected buildings were reconciled by stairs, providing vertical and horizontal circulation throughout the complex.

A sixth-floor office penthouse on the Apex Building was concealed behind the towers on the west facade by means of a setback at the north and south elevations. The years since the original construction had rendered the north wall struc-turally unsound and unsightly; the original sandstone was "face-bedded" (installed with the grain vertical, rather than horizontal as occurs in natural formations), and after decades of freezing and thawing, the stone was peeling. Consequently the wall was rebuilt with concrete masonry backup; a veneer of architectural stone replaced the ashlar wall. The original first floor was turned into a lobby space; the original cast-iron columns were restored and their missing elements replaced. The monumental cast-iron staircase, originally ascending to the second floor, was relocated within the lobby, now descending to the basement-level conference rooms.

The wood Italianate cornices and glass-and-wood storefronts were faithfully reproduced. Wood-framed reproduction windows replaced the damaged originals in all three buildings. The current structure contains the Sears corporate governmental affairs offices, Sears World Trade, and the Sears Financial Center.

RIGHT AND FAR RIGHT: *Interior, during renovation.* The first floor of the old Apex Building became a lobby. The cast-iron columns were restored and their missing elements were replaced.

BELOW: *Interior, after.* The Apex Building, with its plastered brick vaults spanning iron beams on the first floor, was one of the first fire-resistant buildings in Washington.

WHITE HOUSE STATION LIBRARY

WHITE HOUSE STATION, READINGTON TOWNSHIP, NEW JERSEY

FROM: Train station
TO: Public library

TOP: *Exterior, before*. The Romanesque station was built in the 1890s. In its eyebrow dormers and other features it shows the influence of H. H. Richardson.

ABOVE: *Interior, before*. The station had been neglected for many years. New Jersey Transit has a program for leasing such structures to municipalities for adaptive reuse.

In 1979, New Jersey Transit, the newly formed commuter rail system, took a survey of the eleven rail lines it inherited from Conrail to discover the condition of its 144 stations and to suggest possible adaptive reuses for the obsolete and abandoned ones. White House Station was the first New Jersey Transit station to be leased to a municipality and rehabilitated for the community.

At the close of the last century, the Central Railroad of New Jersey had commissioned independent architects to design several new stations along its expanding network. The main line (now known as the Raritan Valley line), reached the town of White House in 1848. Another line, originating in White House, was built in 1888, making the stop a junction between the two lines. The resulting increase in traffic led to the decision by Central Railroad officials to replace the village's existing modest station house. In 1892, architect Bradford L. Gilbert was awarded the commission. The Romanesque station he designed showed the unmistakable influence of H. H. Richardson, whose design for the Auburndale, Massachusetts, station on the Boston-Albany line had been widely published in both popular magazines and trade papers in the 1880s. The exterior design of the station house was distinguished by heavy rusticated stone walls, eyebrow windows (also called eyelid dormers) in the deeply overhanging roof, and a curved portico along the main

street with four pairs of half-height columns.

A 1980 station assessment done by New Jersey Transit rated the structure as having "considerable architectural interest," and the suggestion was made that "the station should be renovated for reuse"—preferably through the New Jersey Transit Station Leasing Program. Under this program, municipalities or other local government entities are responsible for maintaining and operating the station buildings. Extra space within the station is made available for municipal use, subleased to a nonprofit organization, or subleased for commercial use. The income received from rental and parking fees is used to offset the costs of operating and maintaining the station facilities.

When the railroad company informed the Readington Township Committee that it was interested in leasing out the station, a local citizen suggested that the building would make a good library. Since the township had never established its own public library, the proposal was accepted.

Neglected for years, the station was in a poor state. The slate roof needed replacement, together with a rotted window and wall. A well and a new holding tank were essential. The interior, having undergone no architectural redesign since it was built, required a bathroom and a heating system; broken curved glass (specially made, and very costly) had to be replaced, and innumerable layers of blackened shellac had to be

RIGHT: *Interior, after.* The view is from the main library into the children's library, formerly the station's ladies' waiting room.

BELOW: *Exterior, after.* The White House Station Library still serves commuters as a waiting room and opens at 5:30 in the morning for their convenience.

removed from the wainscoting.

Funding for the restoration came in several forms. The leasing agreement gave the township of Readington a twenty-five-year lease for $1. The County Library Board agreed to donate $10,000 for interior furnishings. It also promised to service the branch twice a week and provide the initial stock of books. New Jersey Transit donated $8,000 for site improvements. Readington Township earmarked $15,000 in funds to complete the exterior repairs. An appeal was then made to the citizens of White House, who responded with enthusiasm and generosity. The project was made possible by volunteer labor. Local businesses donated everything from scrapers, ladders, pails, and paint to pizza. Local civic clubs, such as the Jaycees, Rotary, and the Women's Club, held fundraising events. Those who did professional work on the building charged only for materials. A number of private collections were donated to expand the range of books for both children and adults: the collection totals eighteen thousand volumes.

The White House Station Library officially opened on December 17, 1981, seven months after renovation began. A retired local citizen opens the library building each day at 5:30 A.M. to provide railroad commuters with a waiting room where they can read periodicals or check out a book. Through books, the citizens of Readington can now travel the world without ever leaving the station.

MIDWEST

COBBLER SQUARE
CHICAGO, ILLINOIS

FROM: Factory
TO: Rental apartments

From its birth as the Western Wheel Works to its middle age as the Dr. Scholl Manufacturing Company, this twenty-building complex has long been connected with pedal paraphernalia. Set within Chicago's "Old Town" district, in walking distance of Lake Michigan, these factory buildings currently make up Cobbler Square, a residential complex with commercial and support facilities.

The first building of the original Western Wheel Works—a bicycle-manufacturing plant—was constructed in 1889, in a working-class neighborhood. Commercial and industrial expansion characterized this section of Chicago in the late nineteenth century; the Wheel Works followed suit. Architect Henry Sierks designed a second building (1891) to complement his first, both with facades of pressed brick and stone, and vertical and horizontal ranges forming a stately composition. Large areas of each facade were given over to windows, and by varying and recessing their arched heads, Sierks achieved a decorative look.

Another structure was built in 1895 to house the Home Rattan Company. This building, designed by Julius H. Huber and also of pressed brick and stone, blended well with the adjacent buildings. Although it followed the general lines and form of the Sierks buildings, Huber's design expressed more classical features, such as Corinthian-style pilasters rising two and three stories in the main facade and an arched doorway flanked by Doric columns and topped by Corinthian capitals.

Between 1889 and 1895 several additional buildings were constructed in the area between the main structures. Without frontages on public streets, these added buildings were not designed with the same concern for style and composition, lacking the intricate brick stringcourses and the classical and Renaissance features contained in the three major buildings on the site.

As the factory site grew, so did the Wheel Works' reputation. It was the world's largest bicycle manufacturer in the 1890s, at the height of the American bicycling craze. Recreational and competitive cycling clubs were formed and bicycle tours undertaken; Chicago police, ambulance, and municipal workers adopted the bicycle, as did urbanites for commuting and travel, as well as sport. By promoting and sponsoring racers and spending a fair amount of money on advertising, the Wheel Works contributed to this massive surge of popular interest in cycling.

The "safety" bicycle, introduced in the 1880s, made cycling easier and suited to a wider public, both male and female; it replaced the hazardous "Ordinary" bicycle, which had a large front and smaller rear wheel and the rider perched above the high wheel. Schoeninger's models sold as fast as they could be produced. Bicycle news and debates began to fill newspapers, covering issues from local races to the propriety of women riding unaccompanied by gentlemen and the appropriateness of bloomers for the female cyclist. Schoeninger's models—the Blackhawk, Scorcher, Rush, Rob Roy, Juno, and the most popular Crescent—were constantly improved upon; technical innovations marked the Wheel Works plant.

The company president, Adolph Schoeninger, wanted his buildings to reflect the success of his bicycles. He avoided the utilitarian, unadorned nature of many contemporary industrial designs,

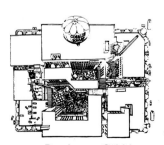

ABOVE: *Rendering*. Cobbler Square.

TOP: *Exterior, during renovation*. The twenty buildings of Cobbler Square are of a wide range of ages, heights, and styles but have been successfully transformed into a unified 295-unit residential complex.

ABOVE: *Interior, after*. The interiors were glutted and many of the structural features were left exposed.

RIGHT: *Exterior, after*. The residential entrance is through a limestone gatehouse to a three-story atrium.

TOP: *Exterior, during renovation.* Some of the buildings in the complex were added as late as the 1950s; they are physically attached to the older buildings but were not nominated for National Register status.

ABOVE: *Exterior, after.* Old granite paving bricks line the courtyard walkways. The complex includes space for restaurants and other commercial facilities.

and displayed through his modern factory the advances he made in manufacturing techniques. And the plant itself served a purpose beyond simply providing shelter for the operation. It also promoted and advertised the business. By creating a unity among distinct buildings, Sierks's designs reinforced the images of immensity in the plant's overall design. Huber's building, with stronger allusions to classical styles, supported this impression of quality, derived from the overall size of the plant and the modern nature of its machines and methods.

By the turn of the century, demand for bicycles began to wane. Americans had transferred their enthusiasm from the bicycle to the automobile, and though Chicago remained the leading manufacturer, production (and profits) dropped considerably. In 1899, in a combination of over thirty major and minor bicycle companies, the Western Wheel Works became a division of the American Bicycle Company. By 1901 the decline of the bicycle business led the American Company to shut down many of its factories and concentrate production in larger plants like the Wheel Works, and also to diversifying its operations into car and car-parts manufacture. Albert A. Pope, an early success with safety bicycles, bought what remained of the bicycle operation in 1903. Pope used the Wheel Works plant as a branch operation, but closed it down prior to 1910.

As the bicycle business left Chicago and the

company Schoeninger built disappeared, another innovative manufacturer moved into the vacant Wheel Works buildings. Dr. William M. Scholl developed a small foot-comfort appliances business into a worldwide industry, making the Wheel Works plant his manufacturing and corporate headquarters. Exploiting his authority as a medical doctor, he extended the foot-care market, set up the Scholl Orthopedic Training School for shoe salesmen to promote Scholl products, and established the Illinois College of Chiropody. Clever salesmanship and a growing awareness of foot problems and their possible relief made Scholl's salves, pads, powders, and supports very popular. Dr. Scholl continued to patent new foot products and add them to his business, which spread throughout the United States and the world.

The Scholl Company occupied the Wheel Works plant from 1911 to 1981, fully utilizing the old buildings and adding new ones in the 1940s and 1950s on adjacent lots. These three- and four-story buildings were constructed of brick and reinforced concrete and have large continuous strips of glass block and windows. They are quite distinct from the older buildings in style and material, and though they are physically attached, they were not nominated for National Register status with the 1890s buildings.

Today, the two-square-block factory site symbolizes a growing Chicago community. Cobbler

BELOW: *Exterior, during renovation.* This 1895 building was designed by Julius H. Huber for the Home Rattan Company. Windows had already been replaced.

Square (named for the more familiar Scholl Company) now consists of 295 residences of varying sizes and shapes. Architects Kenneth Schroeder and Associates removed some of the interior buildings on the site to make way for internal courtyards. Old granite paving bricks from Chicago streets line the courtyards, steel-and-glass walkways adjoin the buildings, and a new three-story atrium (reached by a limestone gatehouse) serves as the residential entrance. The interiors were gutted, while careful attention was given to retaining all original architectural features, such as wood posts and ceiling beams, exposed brick walls, arched doorways, and oversized windows. "Found objects," such as an old Dr. Scholl's store and two boiler houses, were preserved and now add to the diversity of the site. Space was set aside for restaurants, bank services, and drug and grocery stores, as well as recreational facilities for tenants. In every case, the architects attempted to preserve the character of the factory buildings and to modify any intrusive additions made during the course of its history.

From pedaled vehicles to pedal products, this group of buildings should continue to ride on its reputation. In its conversion from one of the largest factory sites in Chicago to the city's largest adaptive reuse project, its distinctive exterior draws attention to the goings-on inside as it did for Schoeninger and Scholl.

THE HELENE CURTIS CORPORATE HEADQUARTERS

CHICAGO, ILLINOIS

FROM: Industrial warehouse
TO: Office building

The Helene Curtis Corporate Headquarters is now located in an industrial warehouse constructed in 1912 and designed by Swedish immigrant Lawrence Hallberg, an architect of both residential and commercial buildings. Situated on Chicago's Riverside Row, it was originally called the John Moir Trust Building, after its owner. The building initially housed eight tenants ranging from a speedometer manufacturer to a shoe-sole maker, a milk-bottle-cap producer, a painter, and a pipe maker. In 1915 the John Stewart and Warner Speedometer Corporation gained ownership of the building. A prolific inventor, Mr. Stewart had as his sole new tenant his own phonograph-manufacturing company. By 1931, the building was owned by Standard Brands Incorporated, which used all nine floors to blend, grind, pack, store, and ship its Manor House brand of coffee beans. Later, 325 North Wells became an annex to the Merchandise Mart and was renamed the Exhibitor's Building. Thirty-three furniture and interior design tenants rented office and showroom space before the building was purchased in 1981.

Under the auspices of the Helene Curtis Industries, a manufacturer of beauty and hair products, the interior of the entire building was gutted, with only the structural system, the brick and stone facade, a stair tower, and parts of the fire protection system left intact. In 1983 rehabilitation began. The architects, Booth/Hanson and Associates, increased the nine floors to ten and added a penthouse level for the extra space required by the company. Triple-layered tinted glass was added throughout the building to screen the sun and block street noise. The green glass

ABOVE: *Exterior, during renovation.* There are now a lounging deck and a boat dock along the river, just outside the employees' dining area.

RIGHT: *Exterior, after.* Green-tinted triple-layer glass screens the sun and blocks street noise.

ABOVE RIGHT: *Exterior, during renovation.* For a period the building was an annex of the Merchandise Mart across the street and was used for exhibition by furniture and interior design firms.

ABOVE FAR RIGHT: *Interior, after.* The lobby dressed in polished marble, is lighted by the same column fixtures that are used on the office floors.

RIGHT: *Exterior, after.* The old warehouse has become a bright new presence along Chicago's River Row and seems ready for another three-quarters of a century of useful life.

blends well with the original red brick walls and their neoclassical detailing. Architect Laurence Booth chose to use green because it complemented both the color of the Chicago River and the metal finishes at the Mart across the street. To maintain a sense of stylistic continuity, the eastern facade was resurfaced with a glass curtain wall, similar in color, that rises through the original roof level.

The new exterior and the story-and-a-half ad-

RIGHT: *Interior, after.* On the office floors, modular work spaces in units of four surround structural columns spaced 20 feet apart. The column enclosures conceal wiring and provide surfaces for indirect lighting.

dition are responsible for the building's bright new presence among other nineteenth- and twentieth-century brick buildings on the river's north bank. But its interior deserves mention as well. The lobby level, which has a view toward downtown Chicago, is dressed in polished marble. Helene Curtis's Beauty Center is located just off the lobby; it develops, tests, and demonstrates new products. The office floors consist of modular work spaces, separated by arched partitions designed by the architects. Units of four work spaces are clustered around large structural columns, that stand twenty feet apart, creating a grid on every floor. These columns also hold light fixtures and computer cables and other wiring. Private offices were constructed on the perimeter of each floor; they have clerestory windows at the tops of their interior walls to allow natural light to reach the open office areas. The glass-walled rooftop addition, partly curved, houses the boardroom, three conference rooms, executive offices, and exercise facilities. A cafeteria for employees is in the basement, just below street level. Outside the dining area, a few feet above the river, is a wooden lounging deck and boat dock. The lower basement houses the building's computer-controlled heating and cooling system, highly unusual in rehabilitated buildings.

The corporate art collection—a variety of images, not as comprehensive as a museum's, but not merely decorative—enhances the building's work environment and unifies the offices floor by floor. Six new tenants will occupy three floors of the completed building. Banners now fly from two flagpoles set atop the tenth story, celebrating the new Helene Curtis headquarters.

ABOVE: *Interior, after.* At the Helene Curtis Beauty Center, just off the lobby, new products are developed, tested, and demonstrated.

RIGHT: *Interior, after.* The Helene Curtis boardroom in the addition has clerestory windows and a framed view of downtown Chicago.

SIX CHIMNEYS
CLEVELAND, OHIO

FROM: Hotel
TO: Apartments for the disabled

Life for the residents of Six Chimneys is vastly different from what it was for former inhabitants. The building once served as a hotel, providing accommodations for, among others, the guests of John D. Rockefeller. Now the structure is home to a special group of adults—mentally retarded, developmentally disabled, or physically handicapped—for whom independent living, even in spare quarters, is a relatively new and unique gift. Walter Zborowsky, executive director of HELP for Retarded Children, spent six years making this project a reality. The building itself was donated to HELP for Retarded Children by Maxine Levin, a devoted Clevelander who among many civic activities chairs the Mayor's Committee for Employment of the Handicapped and the Cleveland Landmarks Commission, and is a trustee of the Cleveland Restoration Society, which she helped to organize.

Six Chimneys, originally six townhouses, was constructed in 1876 by Cleveland merchant Talmadge W. Leek. Built in row fashion (with contiguous frames), they were converted to the elegant Croxden Hotel in 1889. Rockefeller's mansion was located on Euclid Avenue, Millionaire's Row; it was convenient for him to house his guests at the Croxden, situated one block south. Over the years, the building has been known as the Willard, the Pines, and the Reid Hotel. It was the Bascogne Hotel when Mrs. Levin bought it, planning to create apartments for Cleveland State University students.

Mrs. Levin gave up that plan after hitting one too many obstacles. When she hired college students to work on the project, the unions were opposed. She was opposed by a group of prostitutes who believed it was their territory. Then a fire, thought to have been set by a disgruntled former resident, caused $40,000 in damages. When finally some model suites were completed, City Hall refused to grant Mrs. Levin an occupancy permit until the entire building was finished. At this point she decided to give the building to the HELP organization.

The four-story brick building is located in the Upper Prospect Historical Landmark District. It had its exterior restored and its interior entirely renovated thanks to an unusual and hard-won combination of federal, state, and local funds. The six buildings were joined, another floor was added, and several buildings behind were demolished. The original stone floor of the basement remained uncovered; the rest of the interior was gutted and reconstructed to comply with fire code regulations and make it accessible to disabled adults.

The forty-six apartments are occupied by married couples, university students, and individuals working in sheltered employment situations. Tenants may pay up to 30 percent of their incomes for rent and utilities; any balance is paid by funds from the Federal Department of Housing and Urban Development. Facilities for the handicapped were installed, including ramped entrances, wheelchair lifts, elevators, and trouble alarms. The HELP staff provides counseling and training in skills ranging from cooking to money management, so that the tenants can achieve economic and social independence. This was Walter Zborowsky's original intention when the building was donated to HELP, and for the successful realization of his plan, Six Chimneys was awarded

ABOVE: *Interior, after.* A service area. The joined buildings were completely gutted, and the interiors were reconstructed to comply with fire code regulations and to meet the needs of physically challenged residents.

a Certificate of Recognition by the mayor of Cleveland in March 1983.

Zborowsky was also eager to see the prospects for revitalization in this section of Cleveland take root, and they have, in the form of further reinvestments and restoration work. Another benefit, beyond the opportunity for disabled adults to live independently, may be creating diversity in a formerly exclusive, and more recently deteriorating, neighborhood.

ABOVE: *Exterior, after.* There are forty-six apartments, many of them occupied by mentally or physically challenged adults who could not live independently without the services provided by the facility's sponsor, HELP for Retarded Children.

LEFT: *Exterior, after.* The six row houses that compose Six Chimneys were built in 1876 and converted to the elegant Croxden Hotel in 1889. Later other hotels, declining in quality along with the neighborhood, followed the Croxden.

THE OHIO THEATRE
COLUMBUS, OHIO

FROM: Movie house
TO: Performing arts center

ABOVE: *Exterior, before.* Television and the movement from the central city to the suburbs eventually emptied the grand old theater, and the Loew's Corporation closed it.

RIGHT: *Interior, after.* The exits flanking the proscenium are within towering, gilded structures supported by serpentine columns and capped by ornament upon ornament reaching nearly to the star-and-flower-strewn ceiling.

The Ohio Theatre, designed by a leading architect of the movie palace era, Thomas White Lamb, was originally constructed in 1928 as a "presentation house" for silent films and vaudeville shows. Lamb was retained by William Fox, the famous movie house mogul, because of his international reputation as a designer of theaters, including New York City's Madison Square Garden, Ziegfeld's on 42nd Street, and a number of Loew's theaters. Loew's Ohio, as the theater was known, showed movies through the 1940s and early 1950s to full houses. With the advent of television, and the mass exodus to the suburbs following World War II, the Ohio witnessed a drop in attendance, as did most downtown movie houses. Faced with costly upkeep, the Loew's Corporation announced the closing and sale of the grand old theater. In 1969 it was scheduled for demolition.

A group of concerned Columbus citizens rallied to save the Ohio, not simply out of nostalgia but from a larger vision of a performing arts center that would generate new vitality in the ailing downtown center. On March 2, 1969, the Columbus Symphony performed Beethoven's Sixth Symphony to a packed hall; the performance proved that the theater could attract a large audience and that its acoustics were excellent. One reviewer commented that it was "like hearing the symphony for the first time."

The performance brought attention to the theater's plight, and with the attention came financial support. Corporations, local business leaders, and private citizens together gave $2 million to save the structure.

It is indeed a spectacular building. The exte-

BELOW: *Exterior, after.* Behind the curved glass curtain wall of the arts pavilion is a double crisscrossing staircase.

RIGHT: *Exterior, before.* As Loew's Ohio, the theater drew good crowds from 1928, when the fare was silent movies and vaudeville, into the 1950s.

FAR RIGHT: *Exterior, after.* Its restoration completed in 1982, the Ohio Theatre is now the home of the Columbus Symphony and Ballet Metropolitan; it also presents Broadway shows and concerts.

rior is severe and massive; it stands nearly eight stories tall and is decorated with simple pilasters, an opened columned entrance, and blocked-in windows. By contrast, the interior is "as rich an interior as will be found in the country, and with all there is created no feeling of gaudiness," as Lamb described it. Bays with gilded balconies adorn the side walls; each exit is surmounted by a towering, gilded structure, supported by twisted columns and hung with red curtains. Star and flower motifs are strewn across the ceiling. A red-and-gold candlelit chandelier hangs from an eight-pointed star medallion. The entire effect, to modern eyes, is (despite Lamb's claims to the contrary) one of glamorous, atmospheric gaudiness.

To create a workable performing arts center from the movie house, an L-shaped six-story arts pavilion was attached to two sides of the original theater. In this pavilion, designed by the New York firm Hardy Holzman Pfeiffer Associates, are located banquet facilities, expanded lobby, and stage support areas, as well as rehearsal rooms for both musicians and dancers. The architects also added an enlarged orchestra pit, and an orchestra shell, to the original theater to augment acoustics.

The curved glass curtain wall of the arts pavilion reveals a double crisscrossing staircase. Outside the building, an esplanade sheltered by a glass cover shields the walkway and links the theater to a hotel and office complex across the street.

The transformation from movie house to performing arts center has had great success. Completed in 1982, the new Ohio Theatre is now the home of the Columbus Symphony and Ballet Metropolitan; it also presents touring Broadway shows and concerts. While Lamb's other masterpiece, the San Francisco Fox, was lost to the wrecker's ball, the Ohio Theatre lives on, and its continuing triumph has inspired interest across the country in recycling other movie palaces.

BELOW: *Exterior, after.* The Ohio Theatre benefits from the well-kept park across the street.

BELOW: *Interior, after.* "As rich an interior as will be found in the country," claimed its designer, "and with all there is created no feeling of gaudiness." Perhaps, in fact, there is a touch of excess, but genuine glamour, too.

RIGHT: *Exterior, after.* This pavilion was added to house a performing arts center; it is L-shaped, extending around the far side of the theater.

FAR RIGHT: *Interior, after.* The staircase is typical of the grand style of movie palaces of the 1920s and 1930s.

THE MCGREGOR CARRIAGE HOUSE
DETROIT, MICHIGAN

FROM: Carriage house
TO: Architectural office

James McGregor (1830–1909), born and educated in Scotland, was a leader in the American railroad system. After emigrating to Canada, where he secured a job in the car department of the Great Western Railway, in 1860 he ventured to Detroit and soon was made superintendent of the Detroit and Milwaukee Railroad. He became general superintendent of the Michigan Car Works in 1879, and transferred, holding the same position, to the Michigan Peninsular Car Company in 1892. In addition to these industrial interests, McGregor was involved with Detroit's financial community and with the Detroit and Cleveland Navigation Company.

McGregor had the resources to live on East Jefferson Avenue, then "the Queen" of thoroughfares, lined with the mansions of the wealthy. His home was originally a Methodist Episcopal church,

RIGHT: *Interior, after.* The second floor hangs from iron rods attached to heavy trusses, eliminating the need for supporting columns below.

which McGregor bought and converted in 1884. The carriage house, located a distance from the main house, was used for horses and carriages and for storing hay and feed in the second-level loft. It was built in 1885 by A. G. Hollands, mason, and is one of the only four surviving carriage houses on Detroit's East Riverfront. (It also survives the McGregor main house.)

Typical of its time, the carriage house is a common orange-brick Victorian Italianate building. A belfry with paired louvered openings on each of its four sides is centered on top of a pitched roof. A small transverse gable projects from the center of the roof front and back to create a pronounced central bay. The front facade is arranged asymmetrically: a pair of arched four-over-four pane sash windows appears on each story of the east bay, and a single four-over-four window on each story plus an entrance door appear on the west bay. All of the arches have brick voussoirs and stone sills. In the central bay of the front facade was a segmentally arched drive-through opening, with a round-headed casement window centered above the first-story passage. The rear facade was similar to the front, but at some point the central drive-through opening lost its arch.

The "regal" area in which the main and carriage houses were situated fell on hard times in the early twentieth century, because of the rapid commercialization of Jefferson Avenue. Many of the stately homes, including the McGregor house, became tenement buildings. The main house was razed in 1936, and the carriage house was subsequently used as a garage, welding shop, automobile shop, artist's studio, and warehouse.

ABOVE RIGHT: *Interior, during renovation.* The haydrop in the loft was enlarged to become a central atrium.

ABOVE FAR RIGHT: *Interior, after.* The curved glass-block wall screens the front entrance; through it the arched front central opening can be glimpsed.

RIGHT: *Exterior, after.* Built in 1885, the Victorian Italianate carriage house begins its second century of utility, now as the offices of its renovators, Schervish, Vogel, Merz, P.C.

BELOW: *Interior, after.* Flue
and air-conditioning ducts
rise through the atrium.

In early 1981, the architects Schervish, Vogel, Merz, P.C., obtained rights to the building and took four months to convert it into their professional offices. Their first step was to unblock the bricked-up archway in the front facade and fit it with a glass-block S-curve wall, which now serves as the front entrance. They restored the brickwork and added a new roof (originally slate, the roof had been covered with asphalt shingles, which had rotted some of the wooden beams). The interior of the building was substantially altered. A basement was dug for additional office and conference space, and the floor of the first story was raised about 3 feet. The second-story floor was hung from the ceiling beams by iron rods, to eliminate columns on the main floor that would obstruct the space. The architects cut an atrium through the center of the building by enlarging the haydrop in the loft, and a staircase was installed. Exposed ducts—pastel-painted air conditioners—emerge from the atrium, and tubular metal railings surround it on each level. Washrooms and storage modules were situated to cause the least physical change to the original building.

The renovated McGregor Carriage House was given the 1982 Honor Award of the Detroit Chapter, American Institute of Architects. A building grown far from its horse-and-buggy origins—so far that it now has a rear entrance ramp providing access for the handicapped—was successfully adapted by its current tenants and is now the centerpiece of the McGregor Carriage House Historic District.

ABOVE: *Exterior, during renovation.* The brickwork was restored, a new roof was installed, and the belfry (which lights the atrium) was repaired.

RIGHT: *Exterior, after.* The arched drive-through opening was not retained in the rear facade. The building was once an automobile shop and welding shop.

THE CARNEGIE CENTER FOR THE ARTS

DODGE CITY, KANSAS

FROM: Public library
TO: Dodge City Area Arts Council

In 1905, some prominent Dodge City citizens decided it was time their town enjoyed a public library building. With some encouragement from the local women's club, Judge E. H. Madison wrote to the appropriate source: Andrew Carnegie. Carnegie's efforts to promote cultural enrichment throughout the United States began in 1881, when he first provided construction funds for public libraries. Carnegie required that the community locate a building site and collect at least 10 percent of the original donation annually to maintain the facility once constructed. By 1905, Carnegie had provided twelve libraries to Kansas communities, the first to Leavenworth in 1900. In 1905, the Dodge City library board was awarded $7,500 for its building.

C. W. Squires (1851–1934) of Emporia, Kansas, was its architect. At the same time, an active fundraising campaign was launched to secure the $750 needed to operate the library in its first year, and donations of books and materials were solicited. To provide steady funds, the city granted a merry-go-round concession the right to operate in a public park if it would donate 25 percent of its profits to the library fund.

The Dodge City Public Library opened on February 1, 1907. Located at one of the city's main intersections, the two-story building is set on a raised concrete basement, with walls of brick. The center of the building consists of a two-story circular "drum," crowned by a shallow, tiered dome. One-story pedimented pavilions are attached on the east and south sides of this drum, and the main entrance, set into its curved walls, faces diagonally onto the intersection. The second story of the drum and the clerestory of the dome are faced with pressed metal; the cor-

nices are wooden and the roofs sheathed with standing-seam metal. The upper lights of the one-over-one windows are set with stained glass, as are the rectangular single-light windows of the clerestory and drum. The pediments of the shallow pavilions and the frieze on the drum contain insets of decorative metalwork. In 1936, a WPA project provided a one-story addition to the building's west wing, which doubled the size of the building. Stubby finials crown the hip roof of the addition as well as the two original pavilions.

The library's design, accurately termed Free Eclectic style, used classical forms interpreted in such a way as to accommodate other aesthetic and practical requirements. For example, the careful placement of the library on a corner location was intended to make the public building a focal point within its urban environment. It was also one of the few circular, domed structures built using Carnegie funds. The Dodge City Library combined Carnegie's gift toward cultural enrichment with classically influenced public architecture, intended for "civic elevation." The library carried out this weighty task, and also lent books, until 1969, when it moved to new, expanded quarters.

The old library was then empty until purchased privately in 1970, and the Red Palace restaurant was opened there. It next became Casey Jones Junction, a fast-food restaurant until new owners turned it into a private club. Carnegie Hall, Opera House 21, and the Library are the various names this nightclub sported until 1980.

Since 1981, the Carnegie Center has served as an art gallery, artisans' workshop, and headquarters for the Dodge City Area Arts Council. The structure itself was sound; the building had re-

ABOVE: *Landmark plaque.* Communities often take great pride in the success of adaptive reuse projects; Dodge City is no exception.

RIGHT: *Exterior, before.* This photograph was probably made soon after the Carnegie library opened. The circular, domed design is rare for a Carnegie structure.

BELOW: *Exterior, after.* The building now houses the Dodge City Area Arts Council and has served as an art gallery and artisans' workshop.

ceived little maintenance since the 1936 WPA addition. Dodge City architect Eugene A. Gurtner first removed several layers of paint from the metal roof so that water-admitting cracks and holes could be repaired. The concrete-block foundation, which had been severely sandblasted by a previous owner, was also repaired and returned to its original appearance. The deteriorated wood at the windows, the trim, the soffits, and exterior paint were all repaired or replaced. Substantial interior rehabilitation was necessary to suit its contemporary use and meet modern code requirements. Nonhistoric finishes and alterations, such as tile and carpeting, were removed. Painted woodwork was stripped and refinished to match the original clear finish. Water-damaged ceilings, walls, and wood floors were extensively repaired, and new mechanical, plumbing, and electrical systems were installed to replace those that had been in place since the 1930s. The light and airy dome and the WPA addition are used as the Carnegie Center's galleries. The artists' workshop was installed in the basement, and a reading garden is located behind the structure.

The project was completed using a $65,000 grant from the Heritage Conservation and Recreation Service, and $67,000 in nonfederal matching funds. The city once celebrated as "the wickedest little city in the West" for its gunmen and gamblers, dance-hall queens, hustlers, and desperados began its climb to respectability with the women's clubs, library boards, and concerned citizens of the early twentieth century. After its brief interlude as restaurant and nightclub, the library once again houses a much-appreciated cultural institution.

THE WAITING STATION
INDIANAPOLIS, INDIANA

FROM: Waiting place for cemetery mourners
TO: Headquarters of the Historic Landmarks Foundation of Indiana

The Waiting Station of Crown Hill Cemetery originally served as a shelter for mourners. In the horse-and-buggy days, before the introduction of mortuaries and funeral processions, mourners arrived one by one and gathered for warmth and comfort in the Waiting Station until all who were to take part in the service had arrived. They then proceeded to the burial site. The trustees of Crown Hill Cemetery held a competition for the design of the Waiting Station; the winning entry was by the prominent local architect Adolf Scherrer, and was constructed in 1885.

A common feature of Victorian architecture was the use of several different styles in one building, and the Waiting Station is a good example. Romanesque Revival elements are included in the design, such as the massive red brick surfaces, the slender windows with contrasting stone trim, the slightly projecting buttresses, and the entrance arcade set on short, thick columns which give the building mass and a comforting, inspirational air. These are combined with late-medieval French and English elements, such as the finials and decorative brickwork in the gables and in the arches above the windows, to produce a building that gives an impression of brightness and welcome.

By the early twentieth century, the soberly dignified Waiting Station on Crown Hill had outlived its original function. Mourners arrived together in a procession of autos. In addition to this, the city of Indianapolis had expanded northward, which made the trip to the cemetery much shorter. Furthermore, funerals were increasingly being organized by mortuaries. At the same time, Crown Hill Cemetery needed a larger office and depository for its ever-expanding records; Crown Hill is one of the nation's ten largest cemeteries, and one of the very few listed on the National Register of Historic Places. Central heating was installed, and the Waiting Station was used for offices and storage in the following decades. Then, in 1970, plans were approved for a new office building, and demolition of the landmark Waiting Station became a possibility. Eli Lilly, the founder of the Historic Landmarks Foundation of Indiana and a member of the cemetery's board, persuaded the Crown Hill incorporators to lease the building to the Landmarks Foundation for its state headquarters. In return, the foundation agreed to return the Waiting Station to its vintage condition. Mr. Lilly then supplied the considerable sum necessary for restoration, a project guided by H. Roll McLaughlin, FAIA. Work was completed in five months.

The building is sizable. The main hall has a two-story cathedral ceiling and is 30 feet in length with a fireplace at each end. The boardroom, also flanked by fireplaces, extends 20 feet. The main floor holds two large offices, a kitchen, the vault, and rest rooms.

The five original fireplaces were converted to gas logs, the cherry paneling was restored, and the tile hearths were repaired. Gas lighting fixtures replaced the fluorescent tubes that had been used as interim lighting. Seventeen-foot triple mirrors with marble bases now grace the north wall of the main hall, and the old vault is now the accountant's office. Antique Victorian furniture was used wherever possible; Mr. Lilly's father's desk is on display in the executive of-

RIGHT: *Interior, after.* As headquarters for the Historic Landmarks Foundation of Indiana, the building is appropriately fitted with gaslights and furnished with Victorian antiques.

BELOW: *Exterior, after.* The Waiting Station, built in 1885, is a typically Victorian mixture of styles, from late-medieval French and English to Romanesque.

fice. The white-tile cadaver-holding room is now the kitchen, complete with microwave and dishwasher. The basement, once the site of old city heat valves, now houses complete heat and air-conditioning equipment and several brick-vaulted offices that the restoration specialist describes as "spooky."

The bell tower houses the original bell in good working order. It is still rung with a huge rope that ends in the director's office two and a half stories below; it takes two people to pull it. The bell has been rung for the funeral processions of Mr. and Mrs. Lilly, and for one Herbie Wirth—a door-to-door potholder salesman. A letter was found in Mr. Wirth's pocket expressing the fear that no one would attend his funeral. When this became known, over one thousand persons did attend, including a large contingent from nearby Butler University.

The uneasiness new employees of the foundation may feel about their cemetery quarters is soon replaced by the satisfaction of knowing that preservation and restoration are perhaps nowhere more visible than at Crown Hill, and that they are part of a true working restoration, enjoyed by many visitors throughout the year. Visitors still pause here when touring the cemetery, on their way to or from the graves of people such as President Benjamin Harrison, Booth Tarkington, Colonel Eli Lilly, Richard Gatling, and, for those interested in notoriety, John Dillinger.

ABOVE: *Interior, before.* One of the original fireplaces, surrounded by cherry paneling.

RIGHT: *Interior, after.* The two-story main hall, already sizable, is enlarged by the tall triple mirrors.

THE TIVOLI PALM GARDEN
MILWAUKEE, WISCONSIN

FROM: Entertainment hall
TO: Dance studio

ABOVE: *The fire damage.* The roof was gone and most of the floors had collapsed; tar from the roof had melted and run down, staining the walls.

RIGHT: *Interior, after.* The mirrored wall was erected 4 feet behind the storefront windows; it shields the dancers from the street, provides a surface for display of performance publicity and artwork on its other side, and even collects solar heat

What was once the home of one of Milwaukee's Palm Gardens, popular eating, drinking, and dancing establishments, is now quite appropriately the home of another local institution— the Milwaukee Ballet Company. The Tivoli Palm Garden, built in 1901 and converted eighty years later, is located in Walker's Point, one of the earliest urban settlements in Milwaukee and now a historic district. It was constructed across the street from the old Liederkranz Hall, a German theater, in what was the center of a German community originally established in the 1850s. Milwaukee architect Charles Kirchoff designed the building for the Joseph Schlitz Brewing Company. Constructed of "cream city" brick on a limestone base, the building was designed in the Classical Revival style prevalent at the turn of the century. It had a stamped metal cornice and finely tooled masonry; the Schlitz trademark marked its entrance.

During Prohibition the beer garden continued as an entertainment hall, minus the beer, until the building was sold and converted into commercial and office space in about 1943. The original 30-foot ceiling, palm tree murals, and other ornamentation were destroyed in the transition. The building continued to be used for private offices until 1979, when a major fire gutted the structure, collapsing the roof and most of the floors.

The Palm Garden was a key building in a plan to rehabilitate the Walker's Point neighborhood. Early in 1980, a development firm, Carley Capital Group, purchased the building, using a $160,000 grant received through the State Historical Society of Wisconsin. Carley, working with Brust-Heike/Design Associates, developed a plan that would accommodate the studios, dressing rooms, offices,

102

BELOW: *Exterior, after.* The Schlitz trademark still ornaments the pediment. Much of the stamped-metal cornice and fascia was deteriorated, or missing, and has been reproduced in fiberglass or wood.

RIGHT: *Exterior, before.* After a fire in 1979, little remained of the building but the Classical Revival shell of "cream city" brick on a limestone base.

FAR RIGHT: *Exterior, after.* The former beerhall is now the home of the Milwaukee Ballet Company. Its rehabilitation was a major step in the rescue of the Walker's Point Historic District.

ABOVE: *Interior, after.* Careful demolition and painstaking cleaning permitted exposing the brick walls.

and storage needs of the Milwaukee Ballet Company within the shell of the building. The ballet company, founded in 1970, was formerly located in downtown Milwaukee and performed at the Uihlein Hall Performing Arts Center. It operates a ballet school and a community outreach program, and it is considered an important part of the cultural life of its home city and the entire state.

The project was a challenging one, for in addition to the burned-out interior, the architects were faced with a tight construction budget, a five-month deadline, and freezing winter weather in early stages of the work. Steel columns and diagonal bracing were erected to support the south exterior wall before interior demolition could begin and the remainder of the roof and floors could be removed. Leftover plaster and wood lath had to be removed carefully so as not to damage the cream city brick interior. Smoke, soot, and tar that had melted in the fire and dripped down the walls were thoroughly removed.

Another challenge was custom-designing the studio dance floors; extensive research was required. These floors had to have the right amount of resilience for the dancers' needs. By experimenting with the dancers themselves, the architects developed a grid and fastened it to the wood-truss floor system. Two layers of plywood were screwed to the grid. An acoustical steel roof deck and acoustical panels were used in the two-story dance studios to reduce the noise level. An insulated wall was constructed 4 feet inside the storefront windows of the main dance studio; this wall provided the space for practice mirrors and for the display of performance publicity and community artwork. The space between the glass and the wall acts as a passive solar supple-

mental heating system, in which heated air escapes through vents at the top of the wall to warm the dance studio.

Using early photographs of the building, the architects designed the storefront to reflect its original character. It incorporated metal lower panels, large glass fronts, and decorative glass upper panels. Concrete duplicated the limestone in the building's base, matching the decorative shape and tooling of the original. Much of the stamped metal cornice was deteriorated or missing, so intact sections were used to make molds for fiberglass reproductions. A tracing of the remaining metal fascia was made and wood moldings were created to match the metal—a technique both accurate and inexpensive. The globe trademark of the Schlitz pediment at the entrance to the old Palm Garden was restored, repainted in its original colors.

As the Tivoli Palm Garden project neared completion in September 1981, other changes began to appear in the Walker's Point Historic District. Owners of six neighboring buildings restored their storefronts. A major Milwaukee bank within the area restored its building and reopened for business that spring. Through funds provided by the State Historical Society's Federal Preservation Grant as well as the Carley Capital Group/TMB Development Company, the Tivoli Palm Garden Project became a cornerstone in the rescue of the district. The neighborhood is now home to a community of artists, photographers, and dancers, and to some measure reflects its almost-century-old character. From the German polkas of the 1920s to the professional modern ballet of today, the Palm Garden remains a dance lover's haven.

BELOW: A typical interior of one of Schlitz's Palm Gardens (not the Tivoli). The beer stopped flowing with Prohibition, though some of the establishments survived for a while as entertainment halls.

INTERNATIONAL MARKET SQUARE
MINNEAPOLIS, MINNESOTA

FROM: Apparel factory
TO: Regional design center and trade mart

George Munsing and his underwear were big news at the turn of the century. The sleek one-piece union suit of his own design (patented and manufactured in 1891) was a vast improvement over the scratchy red flannel model then in vogue. By 1912, the name Munsingwear was nearly synonymous with underwear—a household word among grateful, comfortable customers across the country.

Munsing might be glad to know that his original manufacturing plant is still in the business of furnishing and marketing designed apparel. Today, however, those designs are intended for homes and offices, floors and walls. The former Munsingwear plant, a five-building factory complex, is now a regional design center and trade mart. Begun in 1983, it is the largest adaptive reuse project ever undertaken by a private developer in the Twin Cities. Over two hundred showrooms were created, in which architects and interior designers can choose furniture and accessories for home, office, and hotel projects.

The original plant was designed by C. A. P. Turner and built between 1891 and 1912. It consisted of four large-scale brick structures, whose exteriors remained unchanged after the renovation. Munsing's plant had a great influence on construction techniques, in addition to his impact on the apparel industry. Concrete construction and an unusual mushroom-column support system were major breakthroughs of the time: poured concrete construction made buildings stronger and more fireproof and reduced costs when compared to the standard combinations of concrete, iron, and steel. This feature was a wonder to the public—that a building could ac-

RIGHT: *Atrium, after.* A restaurant in the courtyard. Steel walkways lining the atrium provide several levels for such facilities.

ABOVE RIGHT: *Exterior, before.* Built between 1891 and 1912, the Munsingwear plant employed poured-concrete construction, which is stronger, more fireproof, and cheaper than the steel or wood framing then standard.

ABOVE FAR RIGHT: *Model.* Kaplan/McLaughlin/Diaz did the planning and design. International Market Square is the Twin Cities' largest private adaptive reuse project.

RIGHT: *Interior, after.* The entrance lobby was formerly a one-story boiler house for generating electricity. The hand-stenciled ceiling ornamentation is original.

tually stand without a steel or wooden framework. The open iron stairway, designed as a double helix and highly detailed and decorated by architect Turner, allows two separate groups to exit from the building's upper floors at the same time without mixing. Because of its style and ingenuity, one architect involved in the project described the stairway as "Sun King" architecture, alluding to the Versailles palace of Louis XIV, and was amazed to find it in a 1905 factory in Minneapolis.

After the success of the union suit, Munsingwear became famous again in the 1950s with the introduction of the first permanent-press (penguin logo) shirts. By the mid-1960s the Minneapolis plant had become the largest integrated knitting mill in the country for men's sportswear. But economic conditions and tough competition (from the "alligator" shirt, for example) forced the plant to close by 1981.

Now on the National Register for Historic Places, the buildings sport one special new feature. A five-story central atrium, formed by the exterior walls of four buildings and topped by a glass roof, is said to resemble an English palm house conservatory. It is circled by steel deck walk-ways, providing different levels for seating and dining. The atrium has also been equipped with speaking and performance facilities; it can be rented out for public events.

The entrance lobby and registration area were moved into an old one-story boiler house. This electrical generating room—a marvel in its time, down to its hand-stenciled designs—now provides access to the whole nine-acre complex. The interiors of the buildings feature high ceilings, large open spaces, original hardwood floors, and decorative ironwork. New corridors and acoustical drywall ceilings were installed within the expansive factory spaces, which were ideally suited for restructuring into a design center.

The project was financed primarily through private investments, though the developers did receive an Urban Development Action Grant and Industrial Revenue Bonds. Architect/planners Kaplan/McLaughlin/Diaz created what they called an "efficient design for the factory complex's profitable reuse." Time will tell if International Market Square will be as great a success, and as innovative, as George Munsing's itchless brand of underwear.

BELOW: *Exterior, before.* The exteriors of the buildings were not changed in the renovation.

ABOVE: *Interior, after.* A wonder at the turn of the century, this double-helix iron staircase still smoothes traffic from floor to floor.

RIGHT: *Atrium, after.* The space, formed by the exterior walls of the buildings, is equipped with speaking and performance facilities and can be rented for public events.

ONE BELL CENTRAL
OKLAHOMA CITY, OKLAHOMA

FROM: High school
TO: Telephone company
state headquarters

One Bell Central, a massive "Collegiate Gothic" building in downtown Oklahoma City, was the first high school in Oklahoma, and is currently the Southwestern Bell Telephone Company's state headquarters.

In 1908, Oklahoma City, which was expanding rapidly at the time, needed a new high school to accommodate its growing student population. Thanks in part to student lobbying, a bond issue for $300,000 was raised to finance the project. The architectural firm of Layton, Smith & Hawk produced the drawings for a four-story limestone-clad reinforced-concrete structure (Layton went on to design seventy-five public buildings in Oklahoma, including the state capitol, the Historical Building, and the Baum Building).

The majestic structure that housed Central High, complete with battlements, bell towers, large pointed-arch windows, and compound-arched entries, features an 85-foot east tower topped with enriched battlements and crowned by cupolas. The building also features an 80-by-70-foot grand auditorium, illuminated by skylights, with a seating capacity of 1,500.

The 1950s and 1960s witnessed several changes in Central High's educational system. It was the first Oklahoma City school to be integrated; it later developed into a vocational learning center with emphasis on technical skills. In 1968 it became a junior high, and eventually was used for an "alternative" school program stressing individual studies and unstructured learning.

The increasing movement to the suburbs in the 1970s, combined with the deterioration of the structure, rendered the school obsolete. With only two hundred students and a decaying building,

the city's only solution was to sell the school. In September 1981, Southwestern Bell Telephone Company's bid of $2.7 million was accepted.

Bell officials were assisted by staff architect Dennis Krost, AIA; Loftis, Bell & Downing; and Frankfurt, Short & Bruza in creating plans for a two-block corporate plaza. Central High was the centerpiece of this "master plan" that included a new data center and support facilities.

Renovation of the exterior proved a challenging task. Wooden window frames were rotting; marble steps were broken, chipped, or long since patched or replaced with concrete. The roof leaked, and the marble walls were damaged in parts. Simply to clean the facade required 1,500 man-hours—it was scrubbed by hand, with soap and bristle brushes.

In the main, the exterior was returned to its original condition. The west entry, however, had to be remodeled to conform to modern access regulations. A matching limestone arch was built; behind it, covering what had been an alley entrance, a glass sheet now hangs. The arch's solid, horizontal mass echoes the shape of the building; the glass sheet provides protection without interrupting the original facade. Lastly, the property was landscaped, and the original 7-foot-tall 250-pound lamps were repaired to dot the patio and entrance walks.

The interior was almost entirely gutted; only what was of architectural significance was kept. The stage and balcony were retained, and the balcony now overlooks several open layers of skylit office space. The refurbished wooden arch from the library, polished, now decorates the executive offices. The old choral room with stepped seating was transformed into a modern seminar room. In the east entry, ornamented by decorative tiles, 1920s Greek murals, and the original marble wainscoting, Bell created a museum of the history of Central High. The air shafts were converted into atriums with glass elevators.

In the process of adapting a national landmark, Southwestern Bell saved themselves an estimated $4 million. The community also benefited, for One Bell Central has brought new vitality to Oklahoma City's downtown and encouraged similar projects in the area.

ABOVE: *Interior, during renovation.* The demolished floors were partially replaced, but a well was left to allow light from above to reach all levels.

RIGHT: *Interior, during renovation.* The central part of the auditorium floor was soon to come out.

BELOW: *Interior, after.* The balcony frieze and the proscenium arch still suggest the bygone auditorium, and the skylights, though plainly glazed, function again.

RIGHT: *Interior, before.* The 1,500-seat auditorium in its prime. The handsome skylight glazing had long gone when the rehabilitation project began.

FAR RIGHT: *Interior, during renovation.* Although the exterior of the old school was largely restored, little of the interior could be saved. Some features of the grand auditorium were retained.

HISTORIC LIBRARY PLAZA
OMAHA, NEBRASKA

FROM: Public library
TO: Offices

ABOVE RIGHT: *Interior, before.* The steel-frame construction, a new technology in the 1890s, permitted considerable freedom in the redesign of the interior and the replacement of the building's systems.

RIGHT: *Interior, after.* The main lobby, with elevator visible through the glass.

Once referred to as the "fading lady of Harney Street," the former Omaha Public Library is again one of the most beautiful buildings in Omaha's central business district. It is among the oldest structures still in use. The origins of the library date to December 31, 1871. That day, a private organization, the Omaha Library Association, was formed to provide the city with its own library. The first library was a small room over a carriage house, where just two thousand volumes were kept. The association never flourished, and a lack of funds forced it to disband in 1877. That year, the Omaha City Council, responding to a new state library ordinance approving publicly funded libraries, levied a tax to fund a new public library, and accepted as a gift all the volumes belonging to the old association. The growth of Omaha's population and the increased demand for books forced the library to move three times, until the need for a permanent facility became imperative.

In 1891, Byron Reed, a real estate entrepreneur, bequeathed land to the city to be used as the site for a permanent library building. Reed also donated his extensive collection of books, manuscripts, and coins. A $100,000 library bond issue was passed that year, and planning began immediately. Thomas R. Kimball, who became one of Nebraska's foremost architects, designed the building in 1892. This was his first major commission, and his drawings were displayed at the World's Columbian Exposition in Chicago in 1893. Among Kimball's other achievements were the Hall County Courthouse in Grand Island and St. Cecelia's Cathedral in Omaha. Kimball was the national president of the American Institute

BELOW: *Exterior, after.* The facade is a good example of Second Renaissance Revival. The portrait roundels on the third story honor classical authors and philosophers.

RIGHT: *Exterior, after.* Thomas R. Kimball designed the library in 1892, the same year the McKim, Mead & White Boston Public Library was finished; the influence is apparent.

FAR RIGHT: *Interior, after.* The library had been vacant for four years when it was sold to Ameritas, Inc., a restoration and development firm, and transformed into offices.

of Architects from 1918 to 1920, and he headed the committee that selected Bertram Goodhue's famous design for the Nebraska State Capitol.

The Omaha Public Library opened on July 5, 1894, with over 48,000 books. As stipulated in Byron Reed's will, the building was designed to be totally fireproof; the structure was erected entirely of steel, stone, and brick. Architecturally, the building is a fine example of the Second Renaissance Revival style. It bears more than a casual resemblance to the most famous building of the Revival style, the Boston Public Library (1888–1892), by McKim, Mead & White. In fact, Kimball lived in Boston when he was a student at MIT, and returned from Paris to found his own firm there in 1888. He was therefore undoubtedly familiar with the design of the Boston building.

The exterior of Kimball's library is decorated with bands of terra-cotta moldings, dividing the pale brick surface into three levels. The windows on the middle level are framed by marble pilasters and topped by rounded pediments, which are filled with floral motif decorations. The names of great authors, such as Goethe, Milton, and Shakespeare, are carved in the entablatures of these windows. On the top level, the windows are separated by terra-cotta roundels with high-relief portraits of ancient Greek and Roman authors and philosophers.

The interior of the old library was not elaborate in design, but it was very diversified in function. The first floor housed a closed-stack book room, as well as the librarian's and cataloguer's offices. Coins, manuscripts, and autographs were placed on the second level, along with reading rooms and a small auditorium. The third floor was often used to display art or ancient artifacts.

This building served the city of Omaha as its main source of public information for eighty-five years. Eventually, the library moved to a larger facility in 1977.

After the old library closed, the building was empty for four years. In 1981, it was sold for development by the city to Ameritas, Inc., a restoration and development firm. With the assistance of architect Larry Reynolds, renovation began on the 34,000-square-foot structure. Renamed Historic Library Plaza, the building has been transformed into office space. The exterior has been left virtually unaltered, except for cleaning and minor repairs. Most of the renovation work has been on the interior, where many original elements have been saved, the most impressive being a bold, ornate iron staircase which encompasses all three floors. Because the original construction used the new steel-frame technology instead of closely spaced masonry walls, the interior has very good spatial flexibility, which allowed replacing all mechanical, plumbing, and electrical systems, and thus meeting new federal, state, and city building and fire codes.

The Omaha Public Library was listed on the National Register of Historic Places in 1978, and the sober countenances of Aristotle, Socrates, Cicero, and Virgil, now preserved, continue their thoughtful watch over Omaha.

ABOVE: *Interior, before.* The ornate iron staircase rises through the second floor to the top.

RIGHT: *Interior, after.* The iron staircase, the most striking of the interior features that have been preserved, helped satisfy the stipulation of the man who bequeathed the land that the building be fireproof.

117

ST. LOUIS UNION STATION
ST. LOUIS, MISSOURI

A soaring clock tower, once the symbol of one of the greatest transportation centers in the world, stood watch over a crumbling symbol of urban decay, the St. Louis Union Station, in 1980. This huge monument to an outmoded means of transportation had grander beginnings. When a consortium of twenty-two railroads decided to construct a new terminal in St. Louis in the late nineteenth century, to replace the tiny old Union Depot, no expense was spared to make it one of the finest anywhere. At the time of the grand opening, on September 1, 1894, the St. Louis Union Station was the largest single-level passenger terminal in the world. The competition-winning design, by St. Louis architect Theodore C. Link, included three main areas: the Headhouse, the Midway, and the Train Shed. The Headhouse—designed in the Romanesque style to suggest a "medieval bastioned gate," complete with turrets—stretches for two city blocks and contained the ticket offices, waiting rooms, offices, and a restaurant. The 11.5-acre Train Shed—the largest ever built—is a steel-and-glass pavilion over 100 feet high that covered the loading platforms and the thirty-one tracks. The Midway was designed as a covered walk, 70 feet wide and over 600 feet long, connecting the Headhouse and the Shed.

Through the first half of the twentieth century, the golden age of rail travel, St. Louis Union Station was the busiest station in the country. By the 1940s over 100,000 passengers came through daily—more than some international airports handle today. But slowly, starting in the 1950s, the public began to choose other forms of transportation. In October 1978, the last train pulled out of St. Louis Union Station.

The original construction costs of this magnificent station had been $6.5 million, a vast sum then, but the Headhouse and especially the Train Shed had deteriorated so far that Oppenheimer Properties, Inc., was able to purchase the buildings in 1979 for just $5 million. A new group, the St. Louis Station Associates, was formed as the official owners, and in 1980 an affiliate of the Rouse Corporation was invited to manage the redevelopment.

To qualify for the 25 percent investment tax credit for historic structures, a necessary key to the development of this National Historic Landmark, it was crucial that all changes meet federal rehabilitation standards. The firm of Hellmuth, Obata & Kassabaum was hired to design a complex of new retail facilities and a hotel, to be combined with the renovation and restoration of the existing buildings.

Almost every building skill and material available had been used in the original construction. The Grand Hall in the Headhouse is being faithfully restored, with its lavish decorations of mosaic, bas-relief, decorative plasterwork, gilt, stained glass, and marble. The hall's high barrel-vaulted ceiling, decorated with intricate stenciling, had been painted over in an earlier attempt to modernize, but is now being uncovered and repaired. The upper section of the walls is made of green scagliola, an imitation marble made of gypsum, adhesive, and colored stone dust, and the lower section is of green faience blocks. Colorful stained-glass windows, set into the decor-

BELOW: *Exterior, before.* The Headhouse of St. Louis Union Station, with the steel-and-glass Train Shed stretching out behind. For decades it was the busiest station in the country, but the last train pulled out in 1978.

RIGHT: *Train Shed, during renovation.* The arched steel trusses will be left exposed. A new six-story hotel structure will extend through the Midway into the Train Shed.

FAR RIGHT: *Exterior, before.* The Romanesque Headhouse, designed to suggest a medieval bastion, contained the ticket offices, waiting rooms, and a restaurant.

BELOW: *Interior, during renovation.* In the Grand Hall the mosaic, stained glass, decorative plasterwork, gilt, and marble are being restored. It will be the lobby of the Omni International Hotel.

ated arches lining the walls, are being cleaned. An allegorical window over the stairs shows three women, each representing one of the main train stations of the 1880s—New York, St. Louis, and San Francisco.

This Grand Hall will become the lobby of the new Omni International Hotel, a 550-room luxury hotel. The Grand Court restaurant will be in the station's original Dining Hall, and the banquet rooms, and approximately one hundred guest rooms, will be located in the renovated Headhouse. A new six-story hotel structure will extend through the Midway into the Train Shed. The shed's roof is being renovated, leaving the original arched steel trusses exposed. Tucked underneath will be three levels of shops and restaurants, set into a landscaped park, complete with plazas, fountains, and a man-made lake. The Midway, with a new wood-and-glass roof, will contain public concourses and areas for exhibits and performances. The original Romanesque arches, along the east and west sides of the Midway, have been uncovered and are being restored.

The $135 million renovation of St. Louis Union Station is one of the country's largest adaptive reuse projects. The magnitude and importance of the project, in addition to the size of its budget, required a high degree of cooperation among the owners, the developer/managers, and the city of St. Louis. That a project of this scope can eventually be brought to a satisfying resolution for all involved parties is another hopeful example.

BELOW: *Interior, grand opening, 1894.* No expense was spared in the lavishly decorated Grand Hall. The construction cost of Union Station was $6.5 million, a huge sum in 1894 dollars.

RIGHT: *Exterior, before.* The shabby block, shown here in the foreground of a 1931 photograph, is now a park.

FAR RIGHT: *Interior, during renovation.* The high barrel-vaulted ceiling, decorated with intricate stenciling had been painted over in an earlier attempt to modernize but is now being uncovered and repaired.

THE TEMPLE APARTMENTS
ST. LOUIS, MISSOURI

FROM: Religious institution
TO: Rental apartments

The developers of the Temple Apartments did not choose the name casually. It accurately reflects the original use, and varied history, of the former B'nai El Temple, built in 1905 and adapted for apartment use in 1982.

By the late nineteenth century, St. Louis had a Jewish population numbering between twelve and fifteen thousand. The B'nai El, a reform congregation, was located on a major thoroughfare in a dense "walking neighborhood," near downtown. It provided religious services and a school for children.

The temple was designed by John Ludwig Wees, who emigrated from Alsace-Lorraine in 1879. His work in St. Louis included prestigious commissions for houses and commercial and institutional buildings as well as more modest stores, flats, and residences. In Wees's plan for this structure, he emphasized the Roman rather than the European or American Christian manifestations of the Romanesque style. The symmetry, the triple-arched entrance portals and window groupings, the twin octagonal towers, the breadth of the facade relative to its height, and the spiraled columns at the entrance allude to the Middle Eastern origins of Judaism.

Located on a corner site, the temple has a rough-faced stone foundation, with walls of red pressed brick, terra-cotta ornament, and stone trim. The three equal arches of the portal rise from spiraled terra-cotta columns and appear below a pent roof whose cornice displays ornamented dentils, brackets, egg-and-dart molding, and corner gargoyles. The round arch form of the entrance is repeated in the windows, the open arcades of the towers, and the corbel tables. The

arches frame stained, and clear, glass roundels that are repeated in the narrower arched windows of the tower and along the sides of the building. Copper and terra-cotta finials crown the towers and gables. The original gray slate remains on some parts of the roof; asphalt shingles have since replaced the rest.

A drawing of the front elevation (published in the *Jewish Voice* in 1904) shows that Wees's plans called for parapet gables to balance the school portion of the structure. On the first floor were the rabbi's study and the director's room (where the fireplace mantels and gas grates are still in use). Above, the organ and choir loft looked out into the temple's upper auditorium, and a gallery supported by iron columns stood above the vestibule. The cove ceiling rose from massive arched brackets above four ornamental columns.

During the 1920s, many members of B'nai El moved to the city's west end. The desire to relocate the temple coincided with the start of the Depression in 1929. While a search was made for a new building, the temple shared its space with the Compton Heights Christian Church. In 1930 B'nai El moved into a church in the west end, and the Compton Heights Church rented the temple for the next fifteen years. B'nai El sold the building to St. Margaret's of Scotland Catholic Church in 1944, and it was used as a parish high school. The school was discontinued after two years, and the parish used the building's two-story central space as a gymnasium and recreation center until 1969. (The auditorium floor originally sloped down toward the rabbi's rostrum and the Ark; it was leveled for this use.) The building was sold to the St. Louis Board of Edu-

ABOVE: *Interior, during renovation.* The architect retained as many features as he could, such as the cove ceiling and the arched brackets.

BELOW: *Interior, after.* This second-floor apartment benefits from the arched windows and vaulting.

RIGHT: *Interior, after.* The bright, high-ceilinged apartments have open-plan kitchens. Some are duplexes.

FAR RIGHT: *Exterior, after.* The building is Romanesque, but is Middle Eastern in feeling; it is unlike the usual European or American Christian Romanesque church architecture.

cation and served for the next six years as the Sherman Branch School; in 1975, it was simply boarded up.

The B'nai El Temple is the oldest surviving structure built by St. Louis Jewish congregations in the early twentieth century. In 1982 it was purchased by the St. Margaret of Scotland Housing Corporation, a neighborhood organization, which found a developer, Mead-McClellan, to convert the temple into apartments. Architect Richard Claybour devised a way to divide the space and still make the most of its architectural details, while installing a second floor. The twenty-eight apartments have high ceilings, much natural light, and open-design efficiency kitchens; three have original fireplaces. The second-floor lofts contain massive carved woodwork, banks of arched windows, and vaulted cathedral ceilings. The largest unit has access to a turret with a view across the city. Bedrooms were set in the octagonal west tower, and in some, spiral staircases lead to loft bedrooms. Uninhibited natural light dramatizes the variously cut spaces.

Architect Claybour avoided damaging the outside of the building because of its National Historic Landmark status, and had to satisfy preservationists and neighborhood residents (whose concern over parking problems led the developer to purchase two adjoining lots to provide extra space), and federal officials (who had to approve the developer's investment tax credits). Rents for the apartments are considered high for the Shaw neighborhood in St. Louis, but everyone seems to agree that preserving the building is important to the area's physical, economic, and historic well-being.

SOUTH

MICHAEL C. CARLOS HALL
ATLANTA, GEORGIA

FROM: Academic building
TO: Museum, classrooms, offices

ABOVE: *Exterior, before*. The hall was built for Emory's School of Law in 1919 as part of a unified campus design by Henry Hornbostel.

RIGHT: *Interior, after*. The hexagonal gallery in the Museum of Art and Archaeology.

In the newly redesigned Michael C. Carlos Hall, one of Emory University's original 1919 buildings, a special exhibition was recently held to inaugurate the school's Museum of Art and Archaeology. It featured the drawings of Henry Hornbostel, who designed the Emory campus, and the drawings and models of Michael Graves, one of today's leading practitioners, and it explored the relationship between the works of the two designers. There could be no better site for this exhibition than the Michael C. Carlos Hall—the result of efforts, sixty-six years apart, by each of these architects.

Emory University was founded in 1914. In July 1915 the university's Building Committee accepted Henry Hornbostel's master plan for the campus. Hornbostel, a partner in the New York and Pittsburgh firm of Palmer, Hornbostel & Jones and head of the Department of Architecture at Carnegie Technical Schools in Pittsburgh, was widely recognized as one of the country's leading architects. His colleagues at the Ecole des Beaux-Arts in Paris called him *l'homme perspectif*, because of his unsurpassable drawing skill. Hornbostel's plan for the campus called for a grouping of buildings arranged with deference to the natural topography, including a central cluster of buildings with two projecting arms, one for the School of Theology and the other for the School of Law. These buildings, with marble-clad exteriors and red-tiled roofs, show the influence of Renaissance Revival and Beaux-Arts architecture. Other major Hornbostel structures on the campus are Dobbs Hall and Winship Hall (dormitories), the Anatomy Building and Physiology Building, and three arched bridges.

TOP: *Exterior, after.* The addition accommodates an entrance and stairwell for the academic half of the building.

ABOVE: *Interior, after.* The Museum of Art and Archaeology has its own entrance in the 1983 addition.

RIGHT: *Exterior, after.* The stair addition on the east facade of the museum.

Although Hornbostel's original scheme for the campus was not fully realized, the university's best architectural features today are still of his creation—with one possible exception: his old law building, which was adaptively reused by Michael Graves. It is now Michael C. Carlos Hall, home of Emory's Department of Art, Department of Archaeology, and Museum of Art and Archaeology. For Graves, the project posed the problem of meeting complex needs for academic use and exhibition space within a moderately sized existing structure. He was able to meet the challenge, while largely retaining Hornbostel's architectural principles.

Graves divided the building in two: one side to house the academic departments and the other to contain the museum. The entrance to the academic half gives the impression of a medieval two-towered facade. Graves abstracted ancient architectural elements to create an effect, "at once mysteriously archaic and Art Deco." In this portion of the building, Graves extended what was originally the law library and divided it into two stories for departmental and faculty offices, classrooms, and a slide library—retaining Hornbostel's tall original windows.

The museum half of the building has its own entrance, a rotunda that reaches into the lobby and echoes the concave curve of Hornbostel's monumental staircase. Hornbostel's large original windows posed problems for the gallery, for they limited the wall space. Graves blocked some windows on the interior, or reduced them to narrow slots, and created an illusion of "excavated space" appropriate to an archaeological exhibition.

Except for the new entrances, the exterior remains faithful to Hornbostel, and along with the grand interior Beaux-Arts staircase, it stands as a reminder of an important period in American architecture, while the building's new design revitalizes it, and suits it, to current needs and ideas.

BELOW: *Interior, after.* The original grand Beaux-Arts staircase marks the division between the museum's two half-floors and the academic departments.

RIGHT, FAR RIGHT, AND BELOW: *Interior, after.* Displays in Emory University's Museum of Art and Archaeology, which occupies part of the renovated Michael C. Carlos Hall.

THE SLOSS FURNACES
BIRMINGHAM, ALABAMA

FROM: Iron production plant
TO: Museum and community center

Until 1871 only the farming crossroads of Elyton, Alabama, marked the future site of the city of Birmingham. But when a railroad crossing was established there, a new town was born. In 1876, James Withers Sloss, son of an Irish farmer, came to this new village from the north of Alabama. A successful business-man and railroad magnate, he joined a small group of entrepreneurs intent on developing industry in Jones Valley. The area was rich in its deposits of iron ore, limestone, and coal—the raw materials needed to produce iron. Birmingham soon became the industrial center of the New South and, thanks to the iron and steel industries, grew dramatically in the bleak period after the Civil War.

Sloss founded the Sloss Furnace Company in 1881, and his two blast furnaces were "blown in" on April 12, 1882. Iron flowed from his plant in great quantities. After Sloss sold the company to a group of financiers in 1886, Joseph Forney Johnson, a future U.S. Senator and governor of Alabama, became president and set the Sloss Iron and Steel Company on a period of rapid expansion, opening two new furnaces in North Birmingham and purchasing extensive coal and ore lands to secure a steady supply of raw materials. In 1888 the Sloss Company bought twelve smaller firms and became the second-largest company in the Birmingham district. The expanded company became known as the Sloss-Sheffield Steel and Iron Company in 1889.

From 1927 to 1931, improved technologies led to some changes at the Sloss Furnace site. The original furnaces were dismantled and replaced by a new pair of steel-encased furnaces, which are the ones currently standing on the site. With the introduction of electricity, many components of the iron-making process were mechanized.

There were more than a few auxiliary machines and structures involved in this process: blowers to pump blasts of air, stoves to heat that air, boilers to produce steam to drive equipment, and a network of pipes, pulleys, runners, and railroad cars to carry steam, water, gases, and raw materials through the system. The Sloss blower building was constructed in 1902 (it is now the oldest building on the site); its steam engines—replaced in 1949 by "turboblowers"—stood over 30 feet high and turned flywheels over 20 feet in diameter. At the other end of the system, in the cast shed, the molten iron was poured into linked shallow molds—which made up a conveyor belt, the "pig caster"—and sprayed with water to cool. When the caster came to the end of its run, the now solid chunks of iron (called pigs) fell into railroad cars, ready to be sold.

The Sloss-Sheffield Company produced pig iron for ninety years, though in its last twenty years it operated under two different names: in 1952 the United States Pipe and Foundry Company purchased Sloss-Sheffield, and in 1969 the Jim Walter Corporation acquired U.S. Pipe and Foundry. The furnaces were closed in 1971, and the Jim Walter Corporation deeded the property to the Alabama State Fair Authority with the hope that it would be preserved as a museum. The State Fair Authority did not feel this plan was feasible and instead proposed its demolition. As a response to that threat the Sloss Furnaces Association was organized by a group of citizens, and through its efforts the furnaces were deeded to the city of

ABOVE RIGHT: *Exterior, before.* When it closed in 1971, the plant was deeded to the Alabama State Fair Authority for preservation as a museum, but the authority proposed demolishing it.

ABOVE FAR RIGHT: *Exterior, after.* A Birmingham citizens' group succeeded in having the furnaces deeded to the city. In 1983, Sloss Furnaces opened as a museum and community center.

RIGHT: *Exterior, after.* A festival in 1984. The center includes an amphitheater for musical performances and, under the water tower, an outdoor stage.

Birmingham. A special bond referendum was passed to raise funds for the preservation and development of the historic property. In 1981 the site was designated a National Historic Landmark, and, befitting its past, it was reopened on Labor Day 1983.

The 30-acre site now serves as a museum of industry (and so of history and culture) and as a community center. The restoration and redevelopment was planned by architect Jim Waters, Jr., and landscape architect Edah Grover. They repaired and repainted the furnaces, added sidewalks, guardrails, and parking facilities, and made other minor improvements to create this true-to-life museum. Its program focuses on tours of the furnace structures; many of the guides are retired blast furnace workers. Exhibitions are held in the old Bath House (once an electrical repair shop and washroom for workmen). It also houses a gift shop and administrative offices, and is the starting point for the tours, which follow the path of raw materials into the furnace and of iron on its way out.

Educational, cultural, and community events take place here as well. The east casting shed was converted into a 1,200-seat amphitheater used for musical entertainment from symphonies to jazz bands to old-time fiddlers. At night the lighted furnace provides a glowing backdrop for the stage. Under the Sloss water tower an outdoor stage was constructed, surrounded by a plaza where visitors can rest or enjoy the entertainment.

Though nothing remains of the very first Sloss furnaces, the 1927 furnaces and the smokestacks, stoves, and cast sheds still cast a powerful presence over the site. No longer toiling under the heat of steam and molten iron, today's visitors may learn about their predecessors, and of their place in the history of the South's foremost industrial city. It is said that the ghost of Theophilus Calvin Jowers, one of the first ironworkers in Birmingham, still haunts the Sloss Furnaces. And it is believed by some that his watchful, righteous eye had a little something to do with the preservation of the furnaces.

BELOW: *In operation.* When the plant was updated to take advantage of new technologies between 1927 and 1931, the original furnaces were replaced by this steel-encased pair.

RIGHT: *Exterior, after.* Guides, many of them former ironworkers, take groups on tours, tracing the path of raw materials into the plant and pigs of iron out of it.

BELOW: *Exterior, before, in operation.* The plant functioned from 1882 to 1971, turning ore into pig iron and contributing to Birmingham's rapid growth as an industrial center.

THE OLD CARROLL COUNTY STONE JAIL
CARROLLTON, KENTUCKY

FROM: Jail
TO: Museum, community groups offices

In 1887, on the Courthouse Square of Carrollton, Kentucky, construction began on a two-story jail, measuring only 20 by 22 feet, to be built entirely of slab blocks of the local limestone.

Thomas A. Boyd of Pittsburgh, Pennsylvania, had initially prepared designs for the jail, but the committee responsible for its construction chose H. P. McDonald & Bros. to provide design and construction services. The walls are 14 inches thick, and floor and ceiling slabs more than 9 inches thick. All interior surfaces of the stone have a rough hammer finish. The windows consist of narrow openings, 3¼ inches wide; even the doors are very narrow, 19½ to 20½ inches wide. Ceiling heights are 8 feet on the ground floor and 6½ feet on the second. The structure is crowned by a wooden hip roof.

This small but forbidding structure was used as the Carrollton County Jail until 1969. Male prisoners were kept on the ground floor and female and juvenile prisoners above. A dungeonlike basement was used for the solitary confinement of the more troublesome inmates.

Soon after it closed, the jail was slated for demolition. The Port William Historical Society convinced county leaders of the landmark significance of the building, and together they decided to seek funds for its conversion.

By the fall of 1983, a $16,000 grant from the Kentucky Heritage Council's Jobs Bill, matched with $17,742 derived from a local hotel/motel bed tax, had funded the project. The renovation program included plans for museum and office space. A Carrollton architect, Douglas G. Robertson, managed to create an inviting interior while leaving the huge limestone slabs completely visible, both inside and out. The existing four cells on the ground floor now contain the Carrollton County Museum, a collection of local memorabilia. The second floor houses the Carrollton County Community Development Corporation, a tourist information center, and offices for civic organizations such as the Chamber of Commerce. The basement, first considered unusable because of its dirt floor and rough rock walls, has now been cleaned, exposing a dry-laid brick floor.

The renovation program involved minimal changes. All stone surfaces were cleaned and left exposed. The only added elements on the ground floor are window glazing and track lighting for display illumination. Mechanical and electrical systems were added to the second floor, as well as six panel doors which were custom-made to fit the 6-foot-4-inch door openings. Fluted door moldings were retrieved from a century-old residential building and added to the interior. The yard, between the building and the iron picket fence, was landscaped to guide pedestrian traffic and add interest and color.

ABOVE: *Exterior, before.* The jail was slated for demolition until a historical society convinced county leaders of its significance and public funds were made available for its renovation.

ABOVE RIGHT: *Interior, after.* The old jail, with its hammer-finish limestone walls, now houses city and county offices, a county museum, and a tourist information center.

ABOVE FAR RIGHT: *Exterior, before.* This forbidding structure was used as the Carroll County jail until 1969.

RIGHT: *Exterior, after.* The 1887 jail measures a mere 20 feet by 22 feet. The windows 3¼-inches wide and the doors approximately 20-inches wide. It now more happily houses local memorabilia and a tourist information center.

1880

Old CARROLL COUNTY JAIL

BRIGHTLEAF SQUARE
DURHAM, NORTH CAROLINA

FROM: Tobacco warehouses
TO: Retail and office complex

The Watts and Yuille tobacco warehouses, named for George W. Watts and Thomas B. Yuille, members of the Duke family, were built between 1900 and 1904 as part of an aggressive building campaign by the American Tobacco Company for storing, aging, and fermenting tobacco for cigarette manufacture. The twin brick structures punctuated the Durham skyline and announced the company's new, bold corporate image, which reflected the flair of its founder, the entrepreneur Washington Duke. Furthermore, the warehouses stood as economic and cultural symbols of the growing importance of cigarette smoking and the industrial revolution's impact on turn-of-the-century America.

The Dukes of Durham are legendary figures in the history of the tobacco industry. In 1865, Washington Duke, aware of the growing popularity of North Carolina tobacco, set up a factory and traveled throughout the state selling tobacco out of his wagon. The enterprise turned into a family one, W. Duke Sons & Co., and soon entered the cigarette-manufacturing market. In an effort to control competition, James Duke combined the nation's largest cigarette manufacturing companies into one: the American Tobacco Company. Thirty-five years after its formation the company controlled 90 percent of the worldwide cigarette business.

The architecture of the warehouses advertised the company's status and reflected its specific functional requirements. The parallel brick buildings with an interior courtyard feature such intricate exterior detail as stringcourses, dentils, pilasters, and elaborate chimneys on the parapet walls of the firewalls. The decorative program precisely articulates the interior subdivisions. Each building is seven bays wide and twenty bays long; the bays are divided by pilasters on the exterior.

The interior of the warehouses was done in post-and-beam construction using two local materials, brick and heart pine timber. Each unit was a large open space 75 feet by 118 feet, with four units totaling 35,400 square feet on each floor, broken only by rows of thick octagonal columns, designed for easy loading, unloading, and ventilating of tobacco leaves. Ten of the seventy-two chimneys were used as vents; the rest are purely decorative.

It has not been possible to assign the warehouses' design to a single architect. Colonel William Jackson Hicks of Raleigh, North Carolina, in an 1897 letter to Benjamin Duke, discussed the practical requirements of the Walker Warehouse he was to build in the area. It is believed that he was responsible for the initial planning of the warehouses, and that Albert F. Hunt of Richmond, Virginia, perfected the plans. Local tradition supports Samuel Linton Leary of Philadelphia, Pennsylvania, who was an active designer in Durham in the 1890s as the architect for these warehouses.

In 1911, the Supreme Court divided the American Tobacco Company into three smaller companies because of its violation of the Sherman Anti-Trust Act. The warehouses were subsequently bought for $4,000 by Liggett & Myers Tobacco Company, which used them for their original function until 1970. The warehouses were then put up for sale. In 1980, private developers, the SEHED Development Corporation, pur-

ABOVE RIGHT: *Exterior, before.* The twin warehouses, built between 1900 and 1904, were used for storing, aging, and fermenting tobacco for cigarettes.

ABOVE FAR RIGHT: *Exterior, after.* The Dukes of Durham did not stint on ornamental brickwork. Ten of the seventy-two chimneys were used for ventilation, but the rest are purely decorative.

RIGHT: *Exterior, after.* Brightleaf Square is within walking distance of downtown Durham and Duke University's East Campus.

137

BELOW: *Exterior, after.* To preserve the appearance of the buildings, store and office fronts are set back from the facades.

chased the buildings for $400,000. Construction began in the spring, and Brightleaf Square opened in November 1981. Its name was taken from a type of flue-cured local tobacco. SEHED engaged Walters, Ferebee and Associates of Charlotte, North Carolina, to adapt these buildings; the project architect was G. Edwin Belk. The buildings house a variety of specialty shops, two restaurants, and offices—Liggett & Myers Tobacco Company even moved its district sales offices back into the renovated warehouses.

Open-air arcades were created in each building facing the courtyard. The south building features two cul-de-sac arcades and an interior corridor. A few new doorways (identical to the original ones) were cut into the courtyard facades, so that every bay now has access to both the street and the courtyard. The store and office fronts are set back from the facades to preserve the architectural integrity of the structures.

The courtyard has been completely redesigned and landscaped; it now contains two entertainment areas and display areas, providing a strong visual link between the two buildings without giving the feeling of insularity common to enclosed suburban malls.

The $6.2 million project is situated at the intersection of Main and Gregson streets, within two primary traffic corridors in downtown Durham. It is within walking distance of the central business district, hotels, and the East Campus of Duke University. Brightleaf Square is targeted to the adult consumer and is intended to serve as a catalyst for the redevelopment of a three-block contiguous area in the vicinity, portions of which are owned by the project's developers.

TOP: *Exterior, before.* The buildings are of post-and-beam construction; each is 7-bays wide and 20-bays long. The pilasters on the exterior indicate the bay junctions.

ABOVE: *Arcade, after.* The courtyard between the buildings links them while providing adequate open space.

RIGHT: *Interior, after.* As well as shops and restaurants, Brightleaf Square contains offices, including district sales offices of Liggett & Myers.

139

SUNDANCE SQUARE
FORT WORTH, TEXAS

FROM: Saloons, hotels, meeting halls, assorted commercial activities
TO: Offices, restaurants, boutiques, galleries, museum

During the late 1800s, Fort Worth was changing from a rural frontier town to a major commercial center. Oilmen, cattlemen, and bankers mingled on Main Street with George Leroy Parker and Harry Longbough (better known as Butch Cassidy and the Sundance Kid). After 1900, stockyards were built that were second in size only to those in Chicago. It was during this period that saloons flourished and Fort Worth prospered with new buildings, fancy hotels, and brick streets that were characterized by their Western style. By the early 1970s, urban blight had taken its toll in Fort Worth; retailers had relocated to the suburbs, buildings were decaying, and the downtown area after working hours resembled a ghost town.

A significant portion of downtown Fort Worth was owned by Bass Brothers Enterprises, a preservation-minded corporation that is based there. In March 1978, after five years of extensive research, Sid Bass announced his company's plans to renew the urban area through preservation rather than demolition. Bass Brothers and the city of Fort Worth applied cooperatively for federal grant money for the revitalization of the central business district. Bass Brothers' pledge to restore the historically significant buildings on Main Street and a commitment to erect a new five-hundred room hotel in the downtown area were the key factors in making it possible for the city to receive a $3 million Urban Development Action Grant.

The results of the Main Street Project, as the preservation effort is known today, are widely acclaimed. Fire Hall No. 1, for example, underwent a careful restoration in 1983 and is now the Fire

RIGHT: *Exterior, after.* A courtyard at the old Plaza Hotel, built in 1908 by Winfield Scott, now provides sheltered outdoor dining.

ABOVE RIGHT: *Exterior, before.* Renovation of the run-down blocks that have become Sundance Square was only part of the Main Street Project for revitalizing the entire urban area.

ABOVE FAR RIGHT: *Exterior, after.* There are no ground-floor storefronts here on the west side of Sundance Square—just trompe l'oeil murals by Richard Haas.

RIGHT: *Exterior, after.* Twelve turn-of-the-century buildings have been restored along the two-block area of Main Street encompassed by Sundance Square.

141

ABOVE: *Exterior, during renovation.* Restoration of the Knights of Pythias building required replacement of those bricks that could not be salvaged with matching bricks from a demolished building in St. Louis.

Hall Marketplace with a museum of Fort Worth history on the first floor and a deli upstairs.

The most impressive accomplishment of the project is Sundance Square, named after Butch Cassidy's sidekick. It encompasses a two-block area on Main Street—the heart of the new downtown area—where twelve turn-of-the-century buildings have been restored. Some of Fort Worth's finest shops, art galleries, and restaurants are now housed in these buildings, renovated by the Dallas architectural firm of Woodward & Associates. Of special note is the Knights of Pythias Building, the first Pythian temple erected in the world, built in 1881. This idiosyncratic red brick building is also where the rotary offset printing press was invented by Staley T. McBrayer in the early 1950s. The turreted three-story structure resembles both a medieval guild hall and a northern European city hall. Today, the first floor is occupied by a women's boutique, and the third floor is available for lectures, civic and professional meetings, and private parties.

Also part of Sundance Square is the Plaza Hotel, built in 1908 by Winfield Scott, one of Fort Worth's leading citizens and most successful businessmen. Opulently decorated with a Moorish influence, the hotel had rooms on the upper floors and a saloon and commercial space on the ground floor. When a courtyard to the south of the building was created in 1979 by removing an unsightly adjoining building, workmen discovered an authentic turn-of-the-century poster nailed to the exterior wall of the hotel, advertising Pawnee Bill's Wild West Show. The poster, now framed, hangs with other memorabilia of the period in Winfield's '08 Restaurant and Bar, which occupies the hotel's first floor. The upper floors contain modern offices.

The City National Bank Building, erected in 1886, was designed by one of Fort Worth's leading architectural firms, Haggart and Sanguinet. The building featured an impressive mansard roof with striking windows and chimneys framing the fourth floor. However, during an "update" in the early 1900s, the entire fourth floor was removed. An integral part of the original building's charm, the fourth floor was completely reconstructed in 1979, using Haggart and Sanguinet's original plans. At the same time, several layers of plaster and paint were removed from the face of the building; matching bricks from a demolished building in St. Louis were used to replace those which could not be saved. The majority of the original bricks were salvageable, however, by a process that required removal and replacement of individual bricks by hand. This same process was used, to a lesser extent, in restoration of the Knights of Pythias Building.

The Weber Building dates back to the 1880s and is believed to be one of the oldest existing struc-

RIGHT: *Exterior, after.* A mural by Richard Haas commemorates Fort Worth's cowboy past. Cattle are still important to the city's economy but so are grain, oil, and the aircraft industry.

BELOW: *Exterior, after.* The Knights of Pythias Building was constructed in 1881, the first Pythian temple in the world.

tures in Fort Worth. During restoration, it was determined that the building was altered around 1915, at which time the original cast-iron columns were removed and transplanted to construct the Bridal Building next door. The Bridal Building was nondescript, whereas the Weber Building truly possessed the architectural detailing and charm of its day. Therefore, the Bridal Building was demolished and its stolen columns returned to the Weber Building for its restoration.

Retail stores, art galleries, restaurants, and small businesses are returning to Fort Worth's downtown. Tourists and corporate relocators are visiting in greater numbers and with greater frequency. The number of conventions has risen dramatically since 1980, and as the developers envisioned, the people of Fort Worth are coming back downtown, too. As for the future—some say it's better than "black gold." Recently, four new skyscrapers have been added to Fort Worth's skyline. The Continental Plaza and the Interfirst Tower each climb nearly forty stories. Paul Rudolph, an architect of international renown, has designed a pair of glass towers, thirty-three and thirty-eight stories high, known as City Center. Sundance Square testifies to the rich possibilities that occur when modern needs and visions are blended with the old. The possibilities continue to grow.

THE ALABAMA THEATRE BOOKSTOP
HOUSTON, TEXAS

FROM: Movie theater
TO: Bookstore

RIGHT: *Interior, after.* Where viewers once stretched their legs and leaned on their elbows, browsers are now invited to scout the bargain-book area.

At its grand opening in 1939, the Alabama Theatre featured Jack Benny playing in *Man About Town.* The marquee announced the celebration for Houston's first suburban movie theater, a sleek Art Deco building, and a welcome addition to the expanding community. With the same celebratory spirit, this time for its preservation, the theater has now been transformed into a bookstore. Although its citizens may miss its movies, they are pleased that the palace will remain.

Behind the Alabama marquee, both sides of the theater (designed by John A. Worley and H. F. Pettigrew) are stepped back in three levels. Neon lights on the marquee light up the eight entrance doors below and the facade above. The building's front is distinguished by a seven-section horizontally banded projection with vertical cutouts on either side.

The exterior, plain but distinctly *moderne*, was unchanged during its renovation. This was a prerequisite for BookStop, an Austin-based discount book chain with stores in San Antonio and Dallas, as well as Houston. The facade was simply cleaned, and a side box office that had been added in the 1950s was removed. The neon signs on the marquee duplicated the original theater signs, but now promote book rather than movie titles. Floodlights illuminate the exterior at night, and "BookStop" has replaced "Alabama" on the marquee.

The interior was more extensively altered, but again its details and atmosphere were maintained by architects and interior designers Chumney/Urrutia. For lack of upkeep, the inside was dingy, the walls were waterstained, the 28-foot

RIGHT: *Interior, after.* Computer books and software have a special section on the mezzanine. The balcony, now closed as a safety precaution, may someday be converted to a coffee or wine bar.

BELOW: *Exterior, after.* The facade was not changed, and the neon signs on the marquee follow the style of the Alabama Theatre's.

ABOVE: *Interior, after.* Book-Stop is an Austin-based discount book chain with stores elsewhere in Texas; this was its first store in Houston.

ceiling leaked, and much of the lighting was inoperable. Repeated remodeling had obliterated some original materials—for example, plywood covers were used over the original curving walls. The new design combined elements of the theater such as the screen and the original ceiling designs and wall murals with innovative space planning.

The lobby contains special book displays and the cashiers' stations, located where the candy counter once stood. The essential *art moderne* details, characterized by rounded, sleek shapes, were enhanced with shades of watermelon, green, beige, and brown paint and floral-patterned Axminster carpeting. The former auditorium now contains the heart of the bookstore. The seats were removed and book stacks installed, using a layout defined by the old theater aisles. The slanted floor was terraced in three places to accommodate the stacks and the browsers. Fluorescent lighting was incorporated into the book stacks, leaving the decorative ceiling medallion and neon cove lights on the walls intact. The wall murals were cleaned and repaired and the screen retained, to be used for projecting images of bestsellers and movie stills. A large newsstand was placed in front of the stage; it carries foreign periodicals and small-press publications as well as

the standard fare. The mezzanine now contains a special collection of computer books and software. The balcony was closed as a safety precaution, though it may someday be used as a wine or coffee bar.

The design used in the alabama Theatre Book-Stop was intended to create a name, or trademark, for the chain, previously unfamiliar in the area (other local branches have since opened). It was also required that the lobby checkout area follow the chain's standard traffic circulation system, and this prevented designer Judith Urrutia from replicating the original symmetry of the lobby—she had gone back to photographs taken in 1939 for this purpose, since it had been remodeled twice since its opening. In modern "retro" style, geometric forms guide the traffic in on the right and out on the left, using faux marbre, plastic laminates, and faux cuir, in green, mustard, and hot pink, to "intensity the environment." The BookStop's architectural and functional origins can still be easily traced, even with its quite flashy new lobby. Having won the Good Brick Award from the Greater Houston Preservation Alliance, the reuse has managed to please the management of the BookStop company, as well as the old moviegoers, who can now escape to adventure not through film but in print.

BELOW: *Interior, after.* The book displays and cashiers' stations in the lobby are in modern "retro" style—the bold, and boldly colored, geometric forms guide traffic in and out.

WARNER PLACE
MIAMI, FLORIDA

FROM: Private residence and
florist shop
TO: Professional offices

This neoclassical house evolved from private residence to office building with scarcely a stud disturbed. The house had remained in the hands of one family since its construction, so little had been destroyed or remodeled over the years. It was also solidly built, so few major structural features needed repair.

Designed by George Pfeiffer, an important local architect who helped start the Florida chapter of the American Institute of Architects, the airy twenty-two-room structure is well lit by its Palladian windows, dormers, lunettes, French doors, and beveled glass sidelights surrounding double doors. Porches with massive Ionic columns, porticoes, a porte-cochère, and balustraded balconies further manifest its expansive Southern-plantation style. The J. W. Warner family left Atlanta for Miami in 1905, coming from a home that had a similar style. The plantation style is adapted to the Florida heat; shady porches and large windows help air-cool the interiors.

The hallways are wide, and the stairwell, decorated with Craftsman-style woodwork, is broad and open. Generously proportioned rooms and large closets, along with unusual materials such as Georgia curly pine paneling for the main hall (the tree is nearly extinct) and coral rock with alabaster for the fireplace, reflect the Warner family's taste for luxury and interest in craftsmanship.

Mr. Warner intended his house to be strong enough to withstand any storm—he had been assistant paymaster of the Florida East Coast Railway when many employees were killed in the hurricane of 1906. The house is constructed of hand-poured concrete, poured by Seminole Indian laborers, aided by donkeys. In 1926, the house's

RIGHT: *Exterior, before*. The concrete walls showed no cracks, unike most Florida concrete buildings of the time; the careful builders did not make their concrete mix with beach sand, which contains corrosive salt.

BELOW: *Exterior, after.* The plantation style was well suited to the humid Miami summers, for in the years before air conditioning, even the wealthy had to rely on shade and natural air circulation for comfort.

RIGHT: *Exterior, before.* The expansive design features porticoes, a porte-cochère, balustraded balconies, pediments, and massive Ionic columns.

FAR RIGHT: *Interior, after.* Features such as the rare Georgia curly pine woodwork in the main hall were intact, but some termite-damaged floors had to be restored.

greenhouse (which was not built of poured concrete) was demolished by the hurricane, justifying Mr. Warner's fears, but the house stood undisturbed.

In 1906, Mrs. Warner began the Miami Floral Company. She moved her business into her newly completed home in 1912. For sixty-six years, this family-run operation continued; all the Warner children worked for it at one time or another, some for most of their lives. As the first floral business in the area, the company developed a clientele which included many prominent early families and businesses, some of whom remained customers for the entire sixty-six years.

The building's distinctive styling, impressive scale, continuity of ownership, and downtown location have made it a designated Miami landmark. It was purchased for restoration and adaptive use in 1972 by private investors.

In 1983, repair work commenced. Concrete porch floors were repoured; the rotting coachhouse doors were replaced; termite-damaged floors were removed, matched, and revarnished; porch stairs and balustrades were repaired. The peeling asphalt dormer shingles were replaced with cedar shingles, in accordance with old photographs of the house. The main porch columns were so well constructed that to this day they show no settlement cracks and needed no repairs. The sand used in the concrete mix for the outer walls was of very high quality, so that the exterior also shows no cracks. Warner Place is one of the few early-twentieth-century homes in South Florida to survive the tropical weather unscathed. Most concrete buildings of the era are made of a mix using beach sand, and the salt corrodes and destroys structural beams.

No major changes were required to turn the building into safe, usable office space. Fire doors were added in inconspicuous locations; sprinkler and fire alarm systems were enclosed in the walls. Air ducts were concealed in closets and behind wallboard. A ladies' rest room was created by removing the common wall in two large first-floor closets. The walls had to be stripped to the studs; the original surface was coated with creosote and covered with cardoard. This material, which is sturdy but no longer considered safe, was replaced with insulated, soundproof wallboard.

The gracious pediment and classic porticoes of the Warner house still look over S. W. Fifth Avenue, though it is now known as Warner Place; the heirs sold it on the condition that the family name be kept. The current owners relinquished rights to alter the zoning or change the facade for the life of the building. With minor repairs and adaptations to modern regulations, this unusual and attractive landmark has made a smooth transition to professional offices. It is now inhabited by lawyers, private investigators, and, conveniently, the Dade County Historic Preservation Division.

ABOVE: *Porch, after.* So solidly constructed was the twenty-two-room house that in three-quarters of a century the columns have shown no settlement cracks.

RIGHT: *Porch, after.* Although the concrete porch floors had to be repoured, the well-built house had deteriorated very little when renovation began in 1983.

SECOND AVENUE NORTH
NASHVILLE, TENNESSEE

FROM: Warehouses
TO: Offices, retail stores, restaurants

TOP: *Interior, before.* Although the old warehouses had never really had an interior, they were extremely solidly built, and original floors and structural members could be retained.

ABOVE: *Interior, after.* In the interconnected buildings from 158 to 174, dramatic light wells have been added to brighten areas distant from the front and rear windows.

Mid-nineteenth-century commercial buildings line Second Avenue North in Nashville, their rear entrances bordering the Cumberland River. No structure rises higher than five stories. Their simple, elegant facades have been preserved on the east side of the street, though the opposite side was greatly altered in 1930 when the avenue was widened.

Over the years, hardware stores, wine and liquor wholesalers, and grocery dealers have occupied the buildings. The proximity of the river was both a help and a hindrance to these businesses. The river wharves behind the warehouses enabled the owners to obtain and store their inventory cheaply and quickly, but the river has also been known to flood. One Nashville resident, Frances Eakes, recalled how during a flood the water rose to her family's second-floor windows, and that her mother could barely get out beneath the arch of the second-floor windows as she left to obtain supplies.

By 1972 the area known as the Market Street Warehouse District was placed on the National Register of Historic Places, one of only two such districts in Nashville. In 1981 several different development firms began to purchase and invest in this area with the goal of remodeling the structures into office space. They hoped that their efforts, combined with the nearby Riverfront Park development, would lead to a revitalized downtown.

Funding for the renovation came both from private investments and from a life insurance long-term mortgage. The cost for remodeling five of the buildings alone (numbers 158 to 174, Second Avenue North) will total $25 million.

As an example of what will be done in the district, the structures from 158 to 174 Second Avenue North will be connected in what R. C. Mathews, Jr., one of the district's major developers, calls a "horizontal high-rise." Behind the old facades, cross-connecting lobbies and corridors now create contiguous office space, which will total 120,000 square feet by the end of 1986. Illumination is provided in part by skylights and light wells. According to Mathews, the buildings were "solidly built to take the weight" of the inventory stored in them, so he was able to retain the original floors; he is "preserving every brick and every structural beam possible" in his remodeling efforts.

The results are striking. Sleek modern oak furniture and white interior walls contrast with the dark nineteenth-century bare-brick outer walls in evidence throughout. The light wells are dramatic, with rows of arched windows lining each floor and echoing the Victorian trim of the facades. Gresham, Smith & Partners was responsible for exterior renovations; Architectural Alliance and Form, Inc., designed the interiors.

Eventually, restaurants and retail shops will line the ground floor on both the Second Avenue and Cumberland River exposures of the structures. Diners and shoppers will be able to look out on Nashville's new Riverfront Park and see all around them the signs of downtown Nashville's rebirth.

TOP: *Exterior, before.* Second Avenue North is in Nashville's Market Street Warehouse District, near the Riverfront Park development; it is hoped that renovation will revitalize the city's downtown.

ABOVE: *Interior, after.* In this conference room the brick was not newly exposed, because it had never been covered; it had only to be cleaned.

RIGHT: *Exterior, after.* These buildings and adjoining ones, from 158 to 174 Second Avenue North, have been connected to form what their developer calls a "horizontal high-rise."

THE JACKSON BREWERY
NEW ORLEANS, LOUISIANA

FROM: Brewery
TO: Retail and restaurant complex

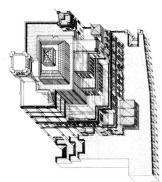

ABOVE: *Conceptual drawing.* The interior was completely gutted, and despite scanty documentation of the brewery's original form much of the exterior was preserved and reconstructed.

RIGHT: *Atrium, after.* View across the atrium from the third floor. Six full-service restaurants and several rooftop terraces draw visitors to the upper levels.

The Jackson Brewery is once again, a functional part of the Vieux Carré in New Orleans. No longer manufacturing Jax beer, it has been transformed into a retail, restaurant, and entertainment complex on the Mississippi River. The Romanesque Revival structure was designed in 1891 by Dietrich Einseidle to resemble the great castles of the beer-brewing capitals of Germany and Austria. Jax beer was a popular favorite for the next eighty-three years, until the brewhouse closed down in 1974. In 1983, Concordia Architects was given the task of preserving Einseidle's exterior, adding a major contemporary addition, and refurbishing the entire interior.

The brewery was originally designed to face the commercial activity on the riverfront. The most elaborate fenestration and millwork were on the river facade, leaving a bare, boxlike exterior on the Jackson Square facade. As Jax beer grew in popularity, the building underwent many alterations and additions, including wood and tin sheds. Enough changes were made, in fact, eventually to obscure the building's original design. As its machinery was updated, interior modifications resulted in the addition of intermediate floors and mezzanines, which left a total of eighteen different levels throughout the structure.

By 1974, the brewery was boarded up—Jax beer could no longer compete with national brands. The building remained vacant until 1982, when a developer who felt the brewery was part of the "emotional fabric of the area" bought it, along with a bordering parcel of public land, to create a mall for tourists and residents. The architects faced numerous problems. The build-

BELOW: *Exterior, after.* View from the river. The brewery was designed to show the riverfront its best faces, and the renovation architects carefully preserved, restored, or re-created them.

RIGHT: *Exterior, after.* A modern six-story building was constructed within the exterior shell; the new structure combines elements of the orignal Romanesque and contemporary features.

ing's entrance faced the wrong way, the floors were of different heights, the structural support system needed repair, several load-bearing walls were not up to the building code, and little documentation of the brewery's original form was available. Because the brewery was situated in the Vieux Carré Historic District, the design had to reflect the area's historic and cultural character and maintain its Romanesque origins yet make clear the distinction between its current and original features.

Because the interior was in such bad shape, and its floors were of eighteen different levels, the architects gutted the building, but they preserved most of the shell. A six-story building was constructed inside this shell, centered around a new 100-foot-high glass atrium. The present interior is all mirrors and neon lights, creating a continuous series of reflections. Elevators, stairs, and mirror-clad escalators carry visitors to the shops around the building's perimeter, where the atrium provides natural light. Pressed-tin ceilings, ceramic tile in traditional patterns, original light fixtures, and ceiling fans were used for nineteenth-century reminders.

On the exterior, the haphazard shed additions were removed and extensive replastering was done. Approximately one hundred wood window frames were replaced, using mahogany. A tower was added to house the elevator, and a new entrance was created on the Jackson Square side. Cream, tan, and light gray with red highlights were used to articulate the facade, and promenades were added around the building. Flood walls had to be built along the Mississippi River (which, according to legend, floods once every century). Rooftop terraces offering various views were created with the hope of drawing visitors to the upper floors of the complex—not always an easy task in vertically arranged malls. People are drawn to the Jaxfest, which occupies the entire third floor and provides all manner of nourishment, from Creole and Cajun traditional foods to foreign specialties. Five full-service restaurants in addition to the Jaxfest are located on the building's upper levels. One, the Brewhouse Café and Bar, is situated in what were the brewery's tank rooms (it still serves Jax beer). Each restaurant offers a view of the building, the river, or the whole district from an open, or glass-enclosed, terrace.

The center was 100 percent leased when it opened in November 1984. A second expansion has begun, to provide more space for retail and other commercial activities. This "festival marketplace," as it is called by the developer, has managed to be both historical and contemporary at the same time, providing continuity with the Quarter's past while serving its current needs. Continuity is also found among the contractors who worked on the brewery's renovation. The Coleman Kuhn Company, surveyors of the property, is the same firm that took part in surveying the original site in 1890, before the brewhouse was even built.

ABOVE: *Exterior, before.* The renovators faced immense problems, among them the constraints of meeting the standards of the Vieux Carré Historic District.

RIGHT: *Exterior, after.* Called a "festival marketplace" by its developer, the Jackson Brewery was fully leased when it opened in November 1984.

WHITEHAVEN
P A D U C A H ,   K E N T U C K Y

FROM: Residence
TO: Interstate tourist center

The traveler crossing over the Ohio River from Illinois is greeted by Whitehaven, a white-painted brick mansion that serves as an interstate welcome center and rest area for the state of Kentucky.

Three prominent Paducah families have owned the house since its construction in the early 1860s. It was originally constructed as a simple two-story brick farmhouse for the Edward Anderson family. In 1903 the house was remodeled in the Classical Revival style by local architect A. L. Lassiter for the Edward Atkins family; the Corinthian-columned portico, elaborate plaster ceilings, stained-glass windows, front entranceway, and main staircase were added, and the stylish mansion was named Whitehaven. In 1908 it was purchased by James P. Smith, mayor of Paducah, and renamed Bide-A-Wee in honor of Mrs. Smith's Scottish background. In later years the house became known locally as the Smith mansion.

The house remained in the Smith family until 1981, but had been empty for thirteen years. During those years, Paducah witnessed the decline of the stately twenty-three-room mansion from neglect and vandalism. At one point, the caretaker's family kept a pony in the kitchen and set up a basketball hoop in the library. There were gaping holes in the brick exterior and severe water damage to the front porch and interior floors and ceilings. One of the six portico columns lay on the ground with its plaster capital shattered. Shutters, plaster molding, stained-glass windows, and marble steps had been pilfered. The house stood on the edge of collapse.

In 1981, a group of concerned citizens from Paducah suggested to the Kentucky Department of Transportation that the proposed Interstate 24 visitor-tourist information center be housed in the Smith mansion. This idea provided an alternative to building a typical rest-stop structure, and the mansion could serve as tourist attraction as well as tourist center. The property was purchased by the Kentucky Department of Transportation, and stabilization efforts began immediately. Restoration began in June 1981, and the house, once again Whitehaven, opened in June 1983. It is the only historic house in America restored as an interstate welcome center. The restoration effort was strongly supported by then Kentucky Governor John Y. Brown and his secretary of transportation, Frank Metts. With federal highway funds administered by the state transportation department, the mansion and the nearby carriage house were restored for $760,000. The construction of access roads and parking lots brought the total project cost to $2 million. This was $800,000 less than the projected cost for constructing a new tourist center.

The architect in charge, J. Patrick Kerr, was committed to restoring Whitehaven to its period of grandeur, and he and project contractor William Black, Jr., strove for a restoration of the highest quality. Original bricks from the house were salvaged and reused to repair the deteriorated exterior brick walls. Period glass was donated by downtown Paducah merchants and installed in the windows; new stained-glass windows now match the original windows. The shattered pieces of the fallen column's capital were carefully glued together, and missing pieces of the plaster moldings and medallions on the ceilings were re-created. Richard Holland, preservation director

RIGHT: *Exterior, before.* The leftmost column lay in the grass, and much of the cornice was gone. There were even gaping holes in the brick walls.

BELOW: *Exterior, after.* Restoration and the construction of new roads and parking lots cost $2 million—little more than two-thirds what a new, and ordinary, tourist center would have cost.

RIGHT AND FAR RIGHT: *Interiors, after.* The restoration consultant, Richard Holland, was able to locate some windows and other features that had been removed, and others were re-created.

BELOW: *Interior, before.* Severe water damage and pilfering had left the house a ruin when the Kentucky Department of Transporation bought it in 1981.

for Paducah Growth, Inc., and consultant for the Whitehaven restoration, was able to locate original mantels, light fixtures, and leaded-glass windows that had been removed from the house. The carriage house was also restored and converted into an office for the maintenance staff.

The individual rooms of the mansion were adapted to meet the needs of the new welcome center. The music room, parlor, and library were restored as museum rooms with furnishings representative of the early 1900s. The dining room, the only area furnished in contemporary style, serves as the information and reception area for visitors. The functional aspects of the rest stop, such as the bathrooms, vending machines, and water fountains, are restricted to the original kitchen wing of the house. The second floor is devoted, in part, to a collection of furnishings, clothing, papers, and historic memorabilia from the estate of Paducah's most famous resident, Alben Barkley, Vice-President of the United States under Harry S Truman.

BELOW: *Interior, after.* The main staircase. On the second floor is a collection honoring Paducah's most famous resident, Alben Barkley, vice-president under Harry S Truman.

RIGHT: *Portico, before.* The house had suffered rain damage and vandalism; the caretaker had a horse in the kitchen and a basketball hoop in the library.

FAR RIGHT: *Exterior, after.* The carefully restored Corinthian-columned portico now welcomes visitors to the inter-state tourist center, which opened in 1983, eighty years after the mansion's Classical Revival remodeling.

THE WARSAW
RICHMOND, VIRGINIA

FROM: Residence; old-age home
TO: Luxury apartments

Having gone through extraordinary transitions in a century and a half, the Warsaw has finally come full circle, as a prestigious private residence. The original three-story, 60-foot-long farmhouse was built in 1832 by William Anderson, a wealthy executive with the Tredegar Iron Works. The lot was purchased in 1830 for $1,750 and the tax on the property was $5.92.

Anderson had been living in Richmond's most prestigious residence, the Belvidere. He chose to build his new brick mansion in the open country, so as to satisfy his passion for extensive gardens and fruit trees. He called it the Warsaw in honor of a Polish friend. After unsuccessful attempts to sell the Belvidere, he decided to rent the Warsaw and move back into his former home. In 1841 the Warsaw passed to Mary E. Gilmer, Anderson's daughter. Her brother-in-law, Thomas Waller Gilmer, was elected governor of Virginia in 1840, and he served as a trustee of the estate. In 1876, the Gilmer children sold the building for $12,500 to James Gibbons, the Bishop of Richmond.

Thereafter, the Warsaw was St. Sophia's Home for the Aged, run by the Little Sisters of the Poor, an order founded in France that maintains charitable hospitals throughout the world.

In 1877, the order incorporated the original farmhouse into a new structure, adding wings to the north and the south, and covered the whole with a new roof and an Italianate brick facade. Elaborate pilasters and ironwork were added, and the building was enclosed within stately Victorian walls. A chapel 40 feet high and 85 feet

ABOVE RIGHT: *Exterior, before.* Although the original residence was built in 1832, almost all of the building, (the entire facade and the mansard roof) was added in 1877 and 1884 to create and expand St. Sophia's Home for the Aged.

RIGHT: *Exterior, after.* The Little Sisters of the Poor moved St. Sophia's to new quarters in 1979, and in 1982 a $5 million project began to convert the Warsaw to thirty-six luxury apartments.

BELOW: *Exterior, after.* The rear of the Warsaw, seen from the former stable, which is now a clubhouse for residents. The complex occupies an entire city block.

long was built to the west of the building. The institution expanded again in 1884. A new wing equal to the size of the whole building was added to the south, and a mansard roof created a full fourth floor. What had been the convent was moved to a new pavilion and the rest was used as a hospital facility. The basement was redesigned to house a large kitchen, laundry, and storage area. Finally a separate structure was added to the west with a community room and guest suite. All the additions were made possible through private gifts to the order.

In 1979, the home moved to a new facility and the Warsaw was abandoned. In 1982, SWA Architects, Inc., of Richmond began a $5 million project to convert the deteriorated Warsaw into thirty-six luxury condominiums. The interior was stripped to the beams, windows that had been sealed shut were reopened, the roof was replaced, and the floors were refinished. The original 10-foot ceilings and carved moldings testify to the glory of the original residence, but modern amenities were added to ensure comfort. No two units are alike. One apartment's master bedroom is located in the apse of the former chapel; a skylight was created from the steeple. The original arched doorways were duplicated for all the entrances and living areas. Classical columns separate large spaces. The old stable was converted into a resident clubhouse, complete with sauna, dressing rooms, and swimming pool. The $5 million project is managed by Area Corporation of Richmond, Virginia.

The Warsaw is situated in Richmond's historic "fan district" within walking distance from the Virginia Museum, the Mosque, and Virginia Commonwealth University. The downtown business and shopping district is five minutes away by car. The complex, situated in a small park circled by its original iron fence, is completely landscaped and occupies an entire city block. Running the course of over a hundred years, the Warsaw once a home for fame and wealth, then a domicile for the destitute, has become luxury housing.

BELOW: *Interior, after.* The renovations respected the original spaces by preserving or duplicating many details and incorporated many up-to-date amenities.

RIGHT: *Interior, after.* A sitting room on the first floor. The iron fence visible in the background was installed by the Little Sisters a century ago and still encloses the landscaped property.

THE SOUTHWEST CRAFT CENTER
SAN ANTONIO, TEXAS

FROM: Convent and academy
TO: Art school, gallery, club

TOP: *Exterior, before.* The Ursuline Academy and Convent in the early 1900s. The former stables and washhouse are now the Club Girard, a private dinner club.

ABOVE: *Exterior, after.* View from the River Garden through the Convent Garden to the first academy structure, built in 1848 of *pisé de terre*—brick handmade from rock, straw, and clay—and covered with stucco.

In the early 1840s, San Antonio was a dying city. Continual wars with Indians and Mexicans had left the town stagnant and virtually deserted. Population had fallen to eight hundred. The missions were in ruins. The only two priests in the city had not said mass in years and were living in open concubinage. Then, in 1842, Bishop Jean-Marie Odin came to Texas to revitalize the Catholic Church. His efforts resulted in the French flavoring of the frontier, particularly in the area of education. Odin's first step was the establishment of the Ursuline Academy and Convent in San Antonio. François Giraud, a newly arrived French architect, was engaged by Bishop Odin to design and supervise construction of the building, which opened in 1851.

Giraud's influence on San Antonio is extensive. He was responsible for the city's public park, only the second in the United States at the time, and supervised restoration of the Alamo. He became city engineer, and ultimately mayor. Unfortunately, with the exception of the Ursuline Academy and St. Mary's College, his architectural work has not survived the ravages of time.

The Ursuline nuns worked, lived, and taught in the academy for over a century. The main building was made in the French *pisé de terre*, or rammed-earth, method: rock, straw, and native clay were compressed into bricks, placed, and then covered with stucco. It was the first time this method had been tried on a two-story building, and the structure remains, with only minor repairs, a fine example of this kind of work. Additional buildings on the site were built in French country style, using native Texas limestone. The tower on the dormitory building holds a three-sided clock, brought over from France in 1868. Driven by two 150-pound weights, it required two nuns to wind it and is still in operation today. Other academy buildings include a fine Gothic-style chapel, designed by Giraud, and the Priest's House.

In 1965, the nuns sold the downtown academy building to the San Antonio Conservation Society and moved to more spacious quarters. In 1971, the society invited the Southwest Craft Center and Art School to move into the old Ursuline Academy, and both institutions were active in raising funds for restoration. The generosity of many individual benefactors played a significant role in that task. Mr. and Mrs. Charles Urschel, Jr., funded the purchase of the dormitory building, and Nancy Negley donated the Cook House. A gift by Mrs. Jack Frost in 1975 allowed the purchase of the remaining Ursuline Academy buildings. Mrs. V. H. McNutt (known affectionately as Momma Mac) found a unique way to celebrate her birthday; she gave a present to the Craft Center each year, including three main gardens and an endowment fund for grounds maintenance. Eventually, through these, and many other, generous contributions, all six buildings were restored and the courtyards and gardens landscaped.

Today, in addition to classrooms and studio space for the crafts center, there are two galleries, a bookstore, and a casual restaurant. The old stables and washhouse have been restored as the Club Giraud, a private dinner club. Dues and proceeds from the club's restaurant provide funds for the preservation of the Ursuline complex and also contribute to the school for handcrafts and art.

BELOW: *Exterior, after.* The dormitory building, built in 1866 and given the clock tower in 1868, houses the executive offices of the Southwest Craft Center and several of its divisions.

RIGHT: *Interior, during renovation.* The Gothic-style chapel 1867. French Catholic missionaries had a far-reaching influence throughout the Southwest.

FAR RIGHT: *Interior, after.* The chandeliers in the chapel were adapted from those in a church of similar age in France.

167

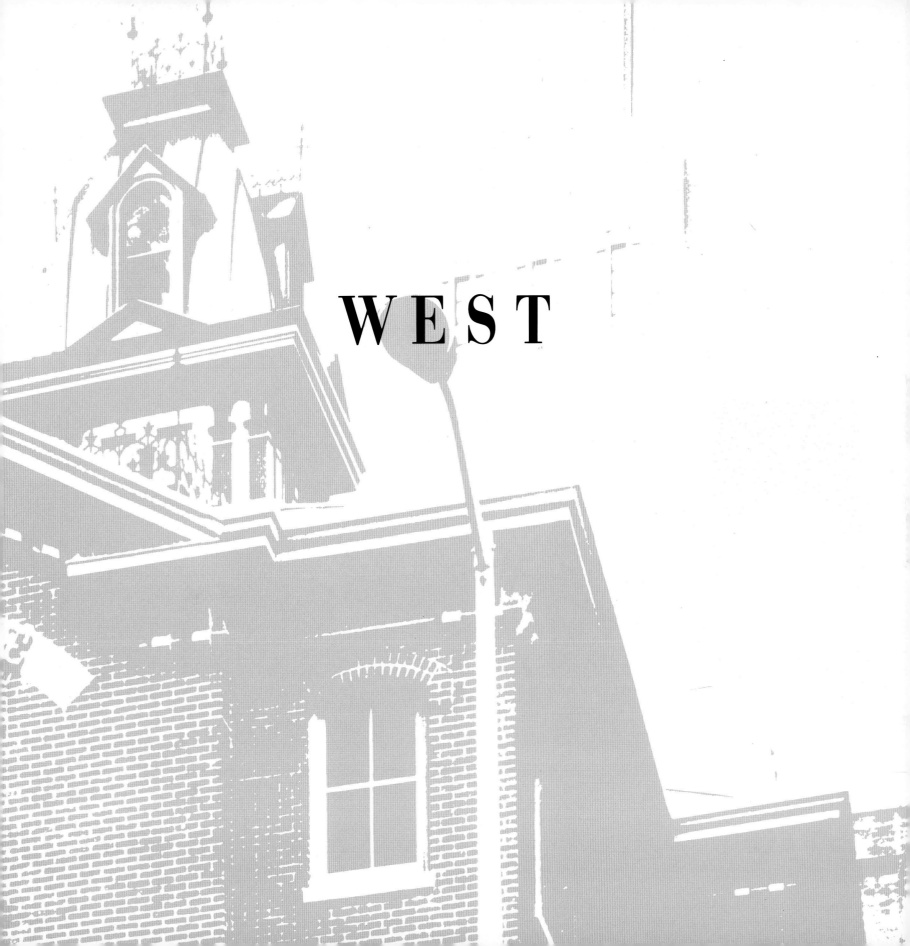

WEST

THE TIVOLI UNION BREWING COMPANY
D E N V E R ,   C O L O R A D O

FROM: Brewing company
TO: Shopping and entertainment complex, office space

ABOVE: *Exterior, after.* The late nineteenth century was an era of ornate breweries and good beer. The Tivoli Union brewers of Denver, a city still known for its brew, celebrated their product with a Second Empire turret.

RIGHT: *Exterior, after.* The complex contains a dozen movie theaters, a dinner theater, several restaurants, shops, and office space.

A Victorian tower crowned the main building of this large industrial complex, while inside, delicate wrought-iron staircases and guardrails crisscrossed the work space. These significant architectural details have been retained, but the years of wear and the accumulated debris are gone. The exterior is now decorated with colorful awnings and shop signs, and large windows display merchandise, not machinery. Shoppers, not laborers, wander along the sidewalks outside.

The Tivoli Union Brewing Company was constructed over the course of several decades: the Brew House in 1882, the Power House in 1930, as well as the Keg House, the Bottling House, and the Fermentation Storage House, for which construction dates are not known. While the buildings had always served as a manufacturing plant, entertainment was not unknown to its bounds: the Turnhalle, a theater connected to the Brewery in 1882, has been a performing arts center since its construction. Nearby, there was a lively, neighborhood corner bar which also served the brewers. Today, these buildings constitute the Tivoli Brewery Redevelopment Project.

The buildings, a short walk from downtown Denver, were among the few saved from a sweeping urban renewal plan that cleared the urban center of most of its nineteenth-century architecture. Although the brewery closed in 1969, the complex was named to the National Register of Historic Places in 1972. It remained vacant until renovation began in 1980 under the direction of Hellmuth, Obata & Kassabaum, P.C. Funding was provided by Trizec Properties of Denver, aided by the 1976 tax act for historic places. The

BELOW: *Exterior, after.* The exterior is now decorated with colorful awnings and shop signs, and large windows display merchandise, not machinery. Shoppers, not laborers, wander along the sidewalks outside.

RIGHT: *Exterior, before.* The brewery was closed in 1969 but was protected from demolition by its National Register listing, and renovation began in 1982.

BELOW: *Interior, before.* The wrought-iron staircases in the Tower Building remain, and some of the copper tanks and other brewing equipment were retained for atmosphere.

Tivoli Brewery redevelopment was the first project to take advantage of this progressive federal legislation.

In the initial phase of the restoration, the rotting interior was cleaned out. The original pipes, railings, and architectural details were left intact as much as possible. Copper brewing tanks were polished to be used as decor in the Brew House restaurant. Elaborate iron trusswork bracing up the cathedral ceiling was brightly repainted, and signs from the former factory, such as "Scale Hopper 280 Bushels," were retained to add to the atmosphere. The original floor plan remains basically unaltered, which allowed the developers to keep most of the staircases and railings.

The finished complex features twelve movie theaters, several restaurants, small retail stores, and some office space.

Out of a factory where men toiled for almost a century to produce beer so that others could enjoy themselves, a mall has been created where visitors can leave work far behind. Yet the details of the original brewery have been saved and transformed, making a charming testament to both honest labor and the history of American industrial architecture.

RIGHT: *Exterior, after.* The Tivoli Union Brewing Company was constructed over the course of several decades: the Turnhalle in 1882, the Brew House in 1890, the Power House in 1930.

BELOW: *Exterior, after.* Both palace of pleasure and monument to labor, the Tivoli complex is only a short walk from downtown Denver.

THE NAVARRE
DENVER, COLORADO

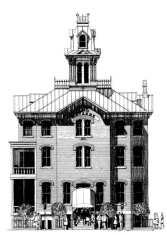

ABOVE: *Exterior, after, line drawing.* The copper-roofed brick structure was built in 1880 as the Brinker Collegiate Institute, a school for young women, but only ten years later had become a hotel and gambling hall.

RIGHT: *Interior, after.* The glass-enclosed stairwell is also a light well, gathering daylight from the cupola.

Located in the heart of downtown Denver, the Navarre has a history as checkered as any of the famous gunslingers who passed through its doors.

Built in 1880 as the Brinker Collegiate Institute, the building passed its first nine years very respectably as a place for young ladies to learn "customary Christian virtues." The young ladies may have gone on to lead virtuous lives; the Navarre did not. Sold to two gamblers in 1890, the building became the Hotel Richelieu. Its fine red velvet draperies created an air of gentility—and also hid the roulette wheel. After only a year, the gambler owners lost the building during a "friendly game" to two other gamblers. This pair renamed the establishment the Navarre, moved the gambling out into the open, and installed a brothel in the upstairs rooms that had been the original girls' dormitory. They also built a short underground railway and linked the basement level with the basement of the Brown Palace Hotel across the street, so that prominent hotel guests could visit the establishment discreetly. One end of the tunnel, complete with rails, is still on display in the lower level of the Navarre. In 1904, Mayor Robert W. Speer told the two owners that the gambling and prostitution had to go. The gambling went, and the downstairs became a fine restaurant; the prostitution stayed, at least until the late 1920s. Though it changed owners several times, the Navarre remained a restaurant until 1963, when it became a private club. In 1974 it was again opened to the public, this time as a jazz club. Renovation projects were attempted in 1979 and again in 1980, but neither was successful. Perhaps the gambling spirit was still

BELOW: *Exterior, during renovation.* Despite its decades as gambling hall and brothel, the Victorian building has a modesty and propriety that shyly but firmly proclaim its origin as a finishing school.

BELOW: *Interior, after.* The stairwell helps illuminate the Remington bronzes. The museum's collection includes works by C. M. Russell, Grant Wood, Georgia O'Keeffe, and other artists inspired by the West.

strong in the old building, because the third time was the charm, and in 1983 the Navarre was sold to William Foxley, businessman and art patron, who that same year managed to turn it into the Museum of Western Art, more than a century after it was built.

The four-story brick Victorian structure has a copper roof. The Victorian detailing was restored, the cupola on top rebuilt, and the interior completely made over by the architectural firm of C. W. Fentress and Associates, P.C., and John M. Prosser, AIA. The maze of small rooms with low ceilings were opened up to create three floors of gallery space, one of office space, and one for the museum gift shop. The front area of the building retains the Victorian character of the early days, complete with period furnishings. The renovation has earned the Museum of Western Art many design awards, including the National Award for Excellence in Adaptive Reuse from the American Society of Interior Designers (ASID) in Chicago.

The Museum of Western Art is one of the few museums in the country to have a building that reflects the historical character of its collection. The permanent collection contains works done by depictors of the American West from the Civil War period onward, including Frederic Remington, Charles M. Russell, Grant Wood, and Georgia O'Keeffe. 1880, the year the Navarre was built, is also important to the history of the West and art—the year C. M. Russell, "cowboy artist," struck out West, and Thomas Moran said the frontier came to a close.

RIGHT: *Exterior, after.* After ninety-odd years of questionable use, the Navarre was sold to art patron William Foxley in 1983 and regained respectability as the Museum of Western Art.

THE FINE ARTS BUILDING
LOS ANGELES, CALIFORNIA

FROM: Space for artists' studios and workshops; offices
TO: Office building

ABOVE: *Exterior, after.* The ornate Fine Arts Center was built to provide studio space for artists, but in 1931, only four years after it opened, it was converted to office space. The supine figures above the third story personify architecture on the left, sculpture on the right.

The Fine Arts Building was erected in the boom period of the 1920s when people and businesses poured into Los Angeles and demanded of architects an appropriate setting for their inward dream of beauty and business ideals. The architects, Walker and Eisen, produced an ornate Romanesque structure accented by generous dashes of Spanish Renaissance design. The ornate Romanesque entrance arches high above decorative bronze doors patterned after those of late medieval Christian churches. The many arches are topped by terra-cotta figures depicting various mythical personages and lounging personifications of architecture and sculpture.

Inaugurated in 1927 with a gala opening that drew 27,000 guests, the twelve-story Fine Arts Building became a haven for artists who rented studio space there. Only four years later, however, the building was sold, converted to office space, and renamed for its successive owners: the Signal Oil Building, the Havenstrite Building, and the Global Marine House.

In 1983, Ratkovich, Bowers & Perez, Inc., a Los Angeles development company, invested $17 million to acquire and restore the Fine Arts Building to its former beauty while bringing the facility up to current office standards. An element central to the restoration was the magnificent two-story Spanish Renaissance entrance lobby. Along its perimeter run high arches of mosaic and terra cotta that rise to the beamed ceiling above the lobby's fountain and tile pool. Centered between the bases of the arches are seventeen tall, ornately pedimented bronze-and-glass showcases that now exhibit art work and thus recall the building's original function. On display is the work of the late noted muralist and decorator A. B. Heinsbergen, whose decorative art is also an integral part of the state capitol in Sacramento, the Los Angeles City Hall, and the Beverly Hills City Hall. The lobby area was refurbished under the supervision of Tony Heinsbergen, son of the original artist, and architect Brenda Levin of Brenda Levin Associates.

Although the fabric of the exterior and the entry lobby of the Fine Arts Building was basically intact, the remainder of the building reflected an anomalous collection of "modern" improvements. Modifications were made in the design of these additions during the renovation to integrate them more fully into the overall design of the original structure.

The building has been completely weatherproofed, the brass entrance doors have been replated and adorned with beveled glass, and plants were introduced at the entrance. A new logo derived from existing detail on the building has been incorporated into terra-cotta plaques commemorating the rededication.

BELOW: *Interior, after.* The two-story Spanish Renaissance entrance lobby is lined with bronze-and-glass showcases that are now used for the display of art, recalling the building's original function.

THE TEMPORARY CONTEMPORARY
L O S   A N G E L E S ,   C A L I F O R N I A

FROM: Warehouses; garage
TO: Museum

On a dead-end street in downtown L.A.'s Little Tokyo neighborhood, in two warehouses which used to be police garages, the first Museum of Contemporary Art, however temporary it was intended to be at the time, opened in Los Angeles in 1983. Originally founded in 1979, MOCA came about because of the combined efforts of national and local cultural and business leaders, together with artists and collectors, to create a new museum where the efforts of distinguished contemporary artists, architects, photographers, and scholars could be experienced and appreciated.

One of the first tasks of the newly formed board of directors was to acquire a building. On land donated by the city of Los Angeles, a plan for an impressive permanent home for MOCA was integrated into the initial phase of a $1 billion California Plaza redevelopment project on Bunker Hill. The planned $22 million structure, designed by the celebrated Japanese architect Arata Isozaki, was slow to start because of protracted negotiations with the developer regarding the site of the museum as well as a downturn in the economy that made financing difficult to arrange. The design process for the museum itself was also somewhat controversial and required time to resolve. With ground-breaking scheduled for mid-1983 and a projected completion date of late 1986, it became apparent that all the interest this new venture had aroused could swiftly fade. The solution was to find MOCA a transitional home.

And so the Temporary Contemporary was established, as an interim exhibition facility, pending completion of the California Plaza building.

ABOVE RIGHT: *Exterior, before.* Residents of the downtown L.A. Little Tokyo neighborhood were puzzled when the project began but now enthusiastically support plans to make the facility permanent.

RIGHT: *Interior, during renovation.* The 1947 warehouse, most recently used as a police garage, had to be brought up to fire, seismic, and access codes but was otherwise little changed.

BELOW: *Interior, after.* In 1984 the Temporary Contemporary exhibited *45°, 90°, 180°/Geometric Extraction* by Michael Heizer, a work most museums and galleries would have difficulty accommodating.

RIGHT: *Exterior, after.* The warehouse loading docks are now the museum's lobby. The temporary quarters of the Museum of Contemporary Art have been so successful that the museum plans to continue to use them even after its new California Plaza facility is finished.

The architect for this challenging $1.3 million renovation, Frank O. Gehry, was an appropriate choice to restore the Albert C. Martin–designed 1947 Union Hardware buildings, since Gehry's own style often employs industrial materials and construction methods. Gehry left the exteriors intact, except for new entrance doors, and built a canopy of chain-link fencing and steel trusses over the newly closed-off street, to form a partially shaded plaza. The interiors were brought up to fire, seismic, and access codes and given

some basic museum appointments. There are two large, open gallery spaces, with a combined area of 55,000 square feet, illuminated by industrial wire-glass skylights and a row of clerestory windows along the south wall. The intricate structural network of steel beams and supports has been left exposed, both serving as support for the many movable display walls and lending a sculptural effect. A steel crane rail, left over from the building's hardware days, remained in place, as removal was too costly. The existing loading docks now move visitors in and out; they serve as the new lobby.

With the comparatively tight budget of about $20 per square foot, the Temporary Contemporary is a fortunate renovation, since Gehry capitalized on the warehouse's resemblance to many artists' studios and achieved an effective exhibition space with minimal alterations. The project took just six months to complete.

A sign of the success of this project is that MOCA has received wide attention and broad membership. Two months after the museum opened in November 1983, MOCA had signed up over fifteen thousand members. In fact, the museum is currently negotiating a fifty-year lease with the city and plans to retain the Temporary Contemporary permanently, even after the move to the California Plaza facility. The Little Tokyo community in which the Temporary Contemporary is located, while initially somewhat puzzled by the museum's interest in the run-down warehouse buildings, has become an enthusiastic supporter of a permanent Temporary Contemporary, citing economic and cultural enhancement of the entire neighborhood.

RIGHT: *Interior, after.* The network of steel beams and pillars, convenient for supporting movable display walls, has a sculptural quality itself.

BELOW: *Interior, after.* The Temporary Contemporary's first show, in 1983, "Painting and Sculpture from Eight Collections: 1940–1980."

GIFTCENTER
SAN FRANCISCO, CALIFORNIA

FROM: Warehouse
TO: Wholesale showrooms
and display facility

The second decade of the twentieth century was a time of changing states. Those who had resisted the modernizing influences of the recent technology boom were shaken by the necessities of an economy geared to finance the Great War, and quickly readjusted themselves to the new reality. It was this sense of economic urgency that led the Eveready Battery Division of the National Carbon Company to commission a new, more efficiently designed building in San Francisco, in 1917. A prominent local architect and engineer, Maurice Couchot, was engaged. Born and educated in France, Couchot moved to California in 1908 and practiced there for twenty-five years, until his death. An early advocate of the use of the latest technology and materials, Couchot worked primarily as a consulting engineer, but either alone or in partnership designed a number of buildings in San Francisco, including the Hotel Canterbury, the Bank of Italy Building, and the Fine Arts Building and French Building at the Panama-Pacific International Exposition of 1915.

Couchot's design for the National Carbon building shows a large-scale industrial structure, overlaid with classical details. Actually two buildings were built around an open courtyard, one fourteen bays and the other fifteen bays long, with large windows in each bay and simple panels dividing the floor levels. At each end of the two elevations are matching doorways with High Style classical detailing, giving the building a more formal appearance. Ornamentation above the doorways included a shield with the initials "NC" and crossed flashlights—the amazing new invention made possible by Eveready's batteries. As a counterpoint to the classical ornamentation, Couchot's structure featured reinforced-concrete construction, a sophisticated ventilation system, a sprinkler system, and an intercommunications network of telephones, pneumatic tubes, and spiral chutes. Built in two phases (in 1917 and 1920), the structures cost $400,000. In 1937, the older portion was acquired by the Blake, Moffitt & Towne Company, an early San Francisco paper-distributing firm, which eventually took over the entire structure in the late 1950s.

In 1981, Blake, Moffitt & Towne vacated the building. A partnership, Buchanan Street Associates, bought it, and began work on its conversion to a wholesale gift market in 1982. The $8.8 million renovation, by Kaplan/McLaughlin/Diaz, Architects, was fashioned to house over 160 permanent showrooms and display facilities, centered around a newly covered 12,000-square-foot atrium which filled in the old courtyard and loading dock. The atrium features balconies on all five levels, retractable skylights, and glass elevators. The space is designed to accommodate special events and includes a stage, kitchens, and sophisticated acoustic and lighting systems.

The interior had historically been unfinished space used for storage, so there was little to salvage from the building's previous uses. The building was structurally upgraded to comply with the new, stricter seismic code.

A fifty-one-block redevelopment project, named Showplace Square, has begun to transform this decaying industrial section of San Francisco into a new design and wholesale trade area. Giftcenter will act as the anchor for future development.

BELOW: *Exterior, after.* The building can accommodate more than 160 permanent showrooms and display facilities. The structure and systems were brought up to code.

RIGHT: *Exterior, before.* California engineer and architect Maurice Couchot built the warehouses for the National Carbon Company in 1917 and 1920, using reinforced-concrete construction and the most advanced systems then available.

FAR RIGHT: *Exterior, before.* The High Style entrances and other classical details modify the extreme regularity of the design. The warehouse was used by a paper-distributing company until 1981; conversion to a wholesale gift market began the next year.

RIGHT: *Atrium, after.* The courtyard between the build-
ings was given a glass roof
and lined with balconies
on all five levels. The project
is part of the larger Showplace Square project to re-
develop fifty-one blocks in
San Francisco's decaying
industrial section.

RIGHT: *Atrium, after.* New Year's Eve at the Giftcenter in 1983.

BELOW: *Atrium, after.* The space is designed for special events and has sophisticated acoustic and lighting systems.

THE ALEXIS HOTEL
SEATTLE, WASHINGTON

FROM: Offices; garage
TO: Luxury hotel

In the heart of Seattle's waterfront district, near Elliott Bay, sits a neighborhood called Waterfront Place, its restoration and construction begun in 1981 and scheduled to be completed in 1986. The Cornerstone Development Company planned this mix of old and new buildings to create an area that would fit well within the existing form of this part of downtown Seattle, a moderate-scale residential and commercial district. Cornerstone designed four new mixed-use buildings to complement the scale and architectural character of the existing structures, most of them dating from the turn of the century, instead of reaching their maximum allowable height and dwarfing their neighbors. Waterfront Place lies between two historic districts, Pioneer Square and Pike Place Market, both multiuse commercial areas. The six buildings included in the restoration project have been listed on the National Register of Historic Places and are designated Seattle landmarks.

Among those six structures is the Alexis Hotel and Restaurant, in what was formerly the Globe Building, built in 1901. It was designed by Max Umbrecht, a prolific early Seattle architect, as an office building and served as the headquarters for various businesses owned by the Clise family, Seattle entrepreneurs. Over the years, various establishments occupied the street-level spaces, including a bank, a drugstore, a fish market, a bowling alley, a restaurant, and other assorted small businesses. The five-story building had masonry walls of tan pressed brick and neoclassical terra-cotta detailing. The south facade held a light court enclosed by an imposing three-story elliptical arch also detailed in terra-cotta.

In the 1920s, the building underwent its first

RIGHT: *Exterior, before.* For half a century the building was the Arlington Garage. By the 1970s the upper floors were disused and only the basement was used for parking; the whole area had deteriorated.

BELOW: *Exterior, after.* Once again the building has a courtyard. The reopened elliptical arch now accents one of the Alexis Hotel's entrances.

RIGHT: *Exterior, before.* In its heyday, the Globe Building, built in 1901, had various commercial establishments along its street level and offices above.

FAR RIGHT: *Interior, during renovation.* Level by level, the roof and floors installed in the 1920s had to be removed.

ABOVE: *Exterior, after.* Terra-cotta details on the facade were carefully restored.

adaptive reuse. The upper floors were gutted and the Arlington Garage, complete with automobile elevator, was created to serve the adjoining Arlington Hotel. At this time the facade's arch was bricked in and the light court was built over at all floors. By the 1970s, though, the upper floors had been closed and only the basement was used for parking. The whole area had deteriorated, leaving many of the buildings underused and in poor condition.

Intending to revitalize this seedy six-block district, Cornerstone planned to convert the old Globe Building into middle-income apartments. When their application for a federal Urban Development Action Grant was turned down, they decided to convert the building into a small luxury hotel instead.

Construction began in the summer of 1981, and the Alexis opened for business about a year later. The exterior of the building was restored with particular attention to its terra-cotta details, such as geometric flourishes at the windows and corners and lion's heads along the cornices. Central to the restoration was the reopening of the arch, which now accents a major entrance to the hotel and frames a landscaped garden court. Ornamental iron balconies and a small roofline pediment were also reconstructed on the primary facade.

The interior of the fifty-four-room hotel is finished elegantly, combining modern and "old world" furnishings. Marble trim was used throughout the building, recycled from other buildings of similar genre in the area. Retail stores selling a variety of items—international books and newspapers, chocolates and crystal, traditional Northwest Indian arts—occupy the street-level spaces. The hotel's restaurant, also served by the archway entrance, has a good reputation, as do smaller meeting places at the Alexis, the Bar and the Mark Tobey, an English-style pub named after the famous American artist, who was born in Seattle. The Alexis has developed a high rate of occupancy and a growing amount of repeat business.

The renovated Alexis was designed by the Bumgardner Architects (Seattle) and won both an award for design excellence from the Seattle chapter of the American Institute of Architects in 1982 and the National Gold Award from the Institute of Business Designers in 1983. In addition to luxury and good design, the Alexis has provided a community service: any person who is in Seattle for treatment of cancer is invited to stay at the hotel with one guest, free of charge, for the duration of the treatment. This humanitarian outreach is arranged through the America Cancer Society and the management of the Alexis.

BELOW: *Exterior, after.* The Alexis is in Seattle's Waterfront Place restoration area, between two other historic districts, Pioneer Square and Pike Place Market. Old and new Waterfront Place buildings will combine to form a mixed residential and commercial neighborhood.

RIGHT: *Interior, during renovation.* When the old Globe was converted to a garage, the courtyard was floored over on all levels.

FAR RIGHT: *Interior, after.* The hotel's restaurant has already earned a good reputation. There are also two bars and a variety of street-level shops to serve both guests and passersby.

THE HIRAM STEVENS HOUSE
TUCSON, ARIZONA

FROM: Private residence
TO: Restaurant

Love affairs, unhappy marriages, attempted murder, suicide, political corruption, gambling, drinking, eviction, and financial ruin are a few of the dramatic activities that have gone on behind this house's simple adobe walls. Today the Hiram Stevens House has been transformed into an elegant restaurant, where diners little suspect the passions that preceded them.

Hiram Stevens came to the Southwest from Vermont, as a soldier fighting the Indians, and stayed as a grocery and provision trader to the soldiers. He was also a notorious gambler. In 1856 he met Petra Santa Cruz, the beautiful daughter of an impoverished second-generation Tucson family. Legend has it that he happened upon her while looking for someone to do his laundry. He spent the next three years trying to persuade her grandmother to let him marry her—difficult because he was a non-Catholic. They finally married in 1859, when Petra was eighteen years old.

The couple spent three years in Vermont; Petra later said she hated the snow and everything else about the state, except that Hiram's mother was very kind to her. They returned to Tucson in 1865, and Stevens built a four-room home, the grandest in Tucson at the time, with 15-foot ceilings. He started a trading post at nearby Camp Crittenden and built Tucson's first hotel, which soon became the finest in the territory.

Stevens s business interests branched out lucratively into mining, sheep raising, and real estate. His most ambitious venture was the Hughes Stevens and Company hardware store. He and his partner, Sam Hughes, who married Petra's sister, Atanacia, sold hardware throughout the en-

ABOVE: *Interior, after.* When it was built in 1865 the four-room house was the grandest in Tucson, with 15-foot ceilings.

tire region of northern Mexico and Arizona. Stevens became involved in local politics and was elected to the state legislature and to the post of treasurer of the city of Tucson. In 1874 he ran for territorial delegate to Congress, turning to his old gambling friends for support; he gave away $25,000 to the most prominent gamblers in the territory, telling them each to bet $1,000 on his winning. If they won, they should return the gift to him and keep their winnings. He won by a handsome majority.

After his defeat for reelection in 1879, Stevens returned to Tucson. He began buying neighboring properties and turning his house into an estate: the property to the north was purchased for rental purposes. Stevens planted an orchard between the two buildings; the property to the east was bought to serve as a driveway for his stables and carriage house; and the property behind his house was used for chicken coops and more stables.

Stevens's businesses began to fail in the early 1890s. He gradually sold off his real estate to pay his debts, and Hughes Stevens and Company headed toward bankruptcy. Shortly after his election as county supervisor, he returned from inspecting a new highway, and went to his room with a headache—his niece recalls that he was often sick at this point in his life, and that the front parlor was used as his sickroom. The story goes that Petra also went to another room to lie down. She awoke to find his hand on her forehead, and then heard a gun go off and felt a burning sensation on her head. She struggled to get the gun away from him; one shot went through her hand, one lodged in the bed. Stevens then

ABOVE RIGHT: *Exterior, before.* Behind the adobe walls the Hiram Stevens family first enjoyed happiness and prosperity; then there were financial troubles, attempted murder and successful suicide, dissipation, disinheritance, and eviction.

RIGHT: *Exterior, after.* The Tucson Museum of Art, given a lease to the property by the city of Tucson in 1968, repaired the exterior and removed false partitions and ceilings added in the 1930s.

ABOVE: *Interior, after.* After renovating the building the Tucson Museum of Art sublet it to the Janos Restaurant; diners sit in comfort where the Stevens family suffered its ruin.

picked up an old army forty-five and shot himself in the forehead. He died shortly thereafter; Petra survived because the Spanish comb she wore deflected the bullet. She inherited little except the Stevens house and an interest in the bankrupt hardware company.

Their adopted daughter Eliza had been raised a "princess," for the Stevenses had been one of the richest families in town. She wore clothes imported from the East, went to the university, and was one of the few girls in town who rode sidesaddle. Unfortunately, the man her mother arranged for her to marry in 1903, Carlos Velasco, was a heavy drinker who gambled away her dowry and left her. She returned to the Stevens home in 1914 with four children.

When her mother died, Eliza was disinherited, done in by what may have been a legal technicality. The home passed into the hands of Petra's niece, Mrs. Knox Corbett. The Corbetts had Eliza evicted, and she was forced to take in sewing to earn her living. In 1918 she bore a daughter by a Mexican who ran a local cigar store, and the daughter took care of her until Eliza's death in 1961. Eliza's brother Thomas, also an adoptee, was a vagabond and drunk; he inherited some

money when his mother died and was never heard from again.

The house is believed to rest on the footings of a wall that surrounded El Presidio, an eighteenth-century Spanish fort built for the protection of the nearby San Xavier Mission. Underneath that wall may lie a prehistoric Indian pit house, but excavations were halted for fear of undermining the foundation of the Stevens house. When the Corbetts inherited the house they rented it out, complete with Petra's furniture and silver. In 1936 the Hoagland Gates family purchased the property—they had recently moved from Maryland and were attracted by adobe architecture. They took down the back porch, built closets, and added false partitions and ceilings. The city of Tucson purchased the property in 1968 and leased it to the Tucson Museum of Art. The museum renovated the building, removing the false partitions and ceilings and replacing the back porch. The Hiram Stevens House, and the Edward Nye Fish House next door (built about 1868), are now both owned by the Tucson Museum of Art. The Stevens house is leased to the Janos Restaurant, where the drinking occurs only in moderation.

THE MANNING HOUSE
TUCSON, ARIZONA

FROM: Private residence
TO: Offices, visitors' and convention bureau

Like many promising young men at the time, Levi Manning set off for the West in 1884, soon after completing his studies at the University of Mississippi. The son of a Congressman, Manning had been raised to a comfortable life and was trained in the various skills a young gentleman needed to make his way in the world. Arriving in Tucson, he was immediately hired as a reporter for a local newspaper, where someone with a quick mind could easily learn the inner workings of a small Western town. Several years later, he worked for the Ice and Electric Company, and rose to be manager. He also served as mineral clerk for the U.S. Surveyor General's office in Tucson for several years. By 1893, Levi Manning was appointed surveyor general for Arizona by President Grover Cleveland, a position he held for four years. For the rest of his life, he was often referred to as "General" Manning.

By 1900, Manning had acquired a considerable fortune and was deeply immersed in mining, commercial, and real estate ventures. He served as mayor of Tucson (1905–1906) after running on an antigambling platform. But his own risk-taking spirit led to two successful enterprises—a commission brokerage house, and a field of oil wells in California.

In 1907 with a new wife, and children on the way, Manning built himself a proper house. He purchased some land at the Santa Cruz Flats, a fertile area near the Santa Cruz River that had been used as pasture and was later cultivated for vegetable gardens by Chinese immigrants who traveled east, as labor for the railroads. Henry Trost, a Tucson architect, designed the Manning residence as a veritable oasis; the 10,000-

RIGHT: *Exterior, after.* When built in 1907 the house was surrounded by 10 acres of park; in vastly expanded Tucson the site is now considered downtown.

ABOVE: *Exterior, after.* The side portico. The masonry-and-stucco exterior shows a mixture of neoclassical and Spanish influences.

RIGHT: *Interior, after.* The Manning House's occupants now include an architectural firm, law firms, and Tucson's Visitors and Convention Bureau.

square-foot single-story structure was set in a 10-acre park filled with trees and gardens. Built for the then enormous sum of $10,000, the house was an idiosyncratic mix of neoclassical and Spanish influences, with a Palladian-style entry, a shaded arcade, and a masonry-and-stucco finish. Round towers anchored the corners of the buildings and the central joining of its two wings. The house became a Tucson showplace and was the site of many celebrated occasions, including the huge garden party given each year on Manning's birthday.

By 1950, after Manning's death, the family no longer occupied the house, and it became the Elks Club's Tucson Lodge 385. The club made three major additions to the structure: a meeting hall, a main dining room, and a recreation room. In the process, the building suffered from some redecoration. In 1979, membership in the Elks had dropped to the point where the club could no longer afford the upkeep, so the building and its grounds were sold to the city of Tucson, which in turn resold the property to the Duraps Corporation, as part of a downtown redevelopment project, with the mandate that it be restored and then adapted to a suitable purpose.

The restoration architects, NBBJ Group/Gresham Larson, were able to return the original residence to its appearance in the year 1920, based on very extensive photographic archives. The original one-story design simplified the installation of new mechanical systems, and the 17-inch-thick walls continue to keep out the searing Arizona heat.

The major new occupants of the Manning House are the Lawyer's Title of Arizona, Tucson's Visitors' and Convention Bureau, an architectural firm, and several attorneys. Tourists can now view the restored section of the Manning House, which has become a focal point for La Entrada Project, an apartment and townhouse development venture by the Downtown Development Corporation (a semipublic authority), mandated to rebuild downtown Tucson.

BELOW: *Exterior, after*. Overgrown shrubbery had to be cleared away, underwatered lawn had to be restored, and the Palladian entrance had to be repaired.

RIGHT: *Exterior, before*. The Manning House was an Elks Club lodge from 1950 to 1979, when membership in the lodge had dropped to the point that the club could not afford the upkeep and sold the house and grounds to the city.

FAR RIGHT: *Arcade, after*. The Manning House has become a focal point for La Entrada Project, a residential development venture by the semipublic Downtown Development Corporation, set up to rebuild downtown Tucson.

ACKNOWLEDGMENTS

My special thanks go to my able assistants, Ada Ferrer and Elizabeth Norton, to whom I owe so much for their part in bringing this book into being, and for their enthusiasm and intelligence throughout the project. And, thanks, too, to Willa Padgett.

This book was made possible by men and women who have chosen to rescue and recycle, to pour their time, energy, or money into the imaginative conversion of buildings that might otherwise have been lost to us and who have thereby added to the architectural flavor and vitality of countless communities.

These men and women have offered me both encouragement and information. Thousands of inquiries went out to landmarks commissions, preservation societies, historical commissions, city planning commissions, individual architects, preservationists, concerned citizens, and state and local arts councils. The cooperation was remarkable and gratifying. Many of the responses to requests for materials came from people who know me through my work; others came from people who don't know me at all, but felt strongly that the subject was sufficiently important to help collect dates, anecdotes, and photographs.

For their efforts on my behalf, as well as their dedication to the broader issues of our mutual concern, including adaptive reuse, I wish to thank the New York Landmarks Conservancy and, in particular, its able executive director, Laurie Beckelman. If you share our commitment to preserving the architectural past, without jeopardizing the future, and would like to be more involved with historic preservation or adaptive reuse, please write to: New York Landmarks Conservancy, 330 West 42nd Street, New York, New York 10036.

And, thanks, too, to Betty A. Prashker, David Groff, Hugh Hardy, Maureen Healy, Richard Haas, Lisa Niven, Lynn Anderson, Oliver Andes, Edwin Belk, Miles Berger, Stephen Bingler, Bruce Blake, Amy Boorstein, Suzanne Brennan, Joanne Brower, Nancy Campbell, Mary Cannon, Maureen Clancy-Solero, Sue B. Courim, Fred Degenhardt, Lydia dePolo, Peggy Dicillo, Virginia Drabbe, Lynn Drobbin, Ellen Flynn-Heapes, Anne Frej, Susan Galford, Rainy Hamilton, Bart Hamlin, Ruth Hamlin, Barbara Harle, Richard Holland, Cynthia Henry, Gerald Jehling, Robert E. Kolba, Peggy Kutcher, Monica Lawrence, Randell Lawrence, Jerry LeBlond, Rania Leon, Bernard Lifschutz, Bert Matthews, Barbara Means, Pierre Moller, Hyman Myers, Michael Newton, Pat Osborne, Katherine Palmer, Marjorie Pearson, Jack Phelps, Allen W. Prussis, Tony Robbins, Douglas Robertson, Ivan Rodriguez, Bernard Rothzeid, Alma Ruiz, Barbara Ryan, Estelle Schneider, Kenneth Schroeder, Pat Sims, Dana Sloan, Carl Spielvogel, Laurie Stark, Leon Sugarman, Nanci Thieme, Jane Thompson, Kathy Ulkus, Elise Urrutia, Joel Wachs, Milt Wackerow, Timothy Wenz, Linda Westfall, Walter Zborowsky.

PHOTO CREDITS

INDEX